LET'S
TALK

LET'S TALK

An Honest Conversation on Critical Issues:
Abortion
Euthanasia
AIDS
Health Care

C. Everett Koop, M.D.
Timothy Johnson, M.D.

ZondervanPublishingHouse
Grand Rapids, Michigan

A Division of HarperCollinsPublishers

Let's Talk
An Honest Conversation on Critical Issues:
Abortion, Euthanasia, AIDS, Health Care
Copyright © 1992 by C. Everett Koop, M.D. and Timothy Johnson, M.D.

Requests for information should be addressed to:
Zondervan Publishing House
Grand Rapids, MI 49530

Library of Congress Cataloging-in-Publication Data*CIP Koop, C. Everett
(Charles Everett), 1916–
    Let's talk : an honest conversation on critical issues : abortion,
euthanasia, aids, health care / C. Everett Koop, and Timothy Johnson.
      p. cm.
    ISBN 0-310-59781-1 (pbk.)
    1. Medical ethics. 2. Abortion. 3. AIDS (Disease). 4. Social
medicine. 5. Euthanasia. I. Johnson, G. Timothy, 1936– .
II. Title.
R724.K65 1992
362. 1—dc20   92–21040
                                             CIP

Edited by Lyn Cryderman
Cover photos by Steve Robb and Jim Whitmer
Cover design by Cheryl Van Andel
Interior design by Bob Hudson

Printed in the United States of America

92 93 94 95 96 /   / 10 9 8 7 6 5 4 3 2 1

Contents

Preface

We first met in the spring of 1987 for an ABC-TV "20/20" profile segment. We knew of each other both in terms of our professional work and our personal religious commitments. But we really got to know each other in a much deeper sense that day, first through a nonstop almost three-hour interview and then through an almost nonstop discussion about life in general and religious convictions in particular as we went to the White House Correspondents' dinner that evening.

Our discussions have continued and our friendship has deepened. We have come to respect and love each other even as we have learned that we disagree on many specific subjects relating to medical ethics. However, we would both acknowledge that we have learned from each other, and that we have grown in our understanding of the human condition because of each other. We also agree that too often persons of opposing viewpoints conclude that there is room in God's love for only one of them. We write this book to demonstrate otherwise; to suggest that it is possible to disagree, sometimes vigorously, and yet acknowledge that God loves us all even while we are all less than perfect in this human pilgrimage.

Several summers ago, we engaged in a week-long series of dialogues at the Pilgrim Pines Conference Center at Lake Swanzey, New Hampshire. Those verbal exchanges were very lively—with much audience participation—and demonstrated the spirit that we hope to convey in this book. Many of the participants in that week—and in several similar sessions we have done since—suggested that we "write a book" that would convey the substance and spirit of those dialogues.

And so this book, a series of letters written back and forth on four of the most critical yet divisive ethical issues facing us today. We trust you will find them useful in forming your own ideas and, more important, in learning to be open to viewpoints other than your own. As letters, they are brief and limited in scope. We do not pretend that they are carefully reasoned essays. They simply represent the kind of give-and-take that often occurs in real-life situations—personal conversations, dinner table talk, or small group discussions.

We should explain the references to the Bible and the teachings of Jesus in our letters. For both of us, the Bible is the primary source of guidance in daily living. And we both see the life and teachings of Jesus as an inspiring model for compassion and courage. However, we recognize that others of you have found different sources of inspiration and we invite you to listen to our viewpoints with an open mind, just as we would do in listening to you.

We hope that you will use this short book to generate helpful discussion and debate among your circle of friends and family. And we hope that if you disagree, you will learn from each other's viewpoints and respect those who differ with you.

Let's talk.

Let's Talk

Many are asking,
"Who can show us any good?"
Let the light of your face
shine upon us, O LORD.
PSALM 4:6

1
Abortion

Dear Chick,

Let's start right off with abortion since that's the issue that still most separates us, and certainly the one with which you were most identified in your public life prior to becoming Surgeon General.

And I choose to begin at what I suspect you will regard as a dangerous point, namely, that whatever else abortion is as an issue, it is also a medical issue. When a woman decides she wants or needs an abortion, she is also deciding that she wants to change her body. Put bluntly, she wants to get rid of something in her body—albeit a very special "something"—that she has decided will do her and/or her family more harm than good. And if we could view an abortion as simply the procedure designed to correct a *physical* problem in a woman's body—*which of course we cannot and should not*—we would then view abortion as a relatively simple and safe medical procedure. Furthermore, we would be appalled at the prospect of a woman's being forced to accomplish this relatively simple medical procedure in an unsafe manner. But the issue of abortion *is* more than a medical issue, and therein, I know, will lie the many differences between us.

As you know, Chick, I often try to find a reasoned middle ground, even on an emotional issue like abortion. Therefore, it will not surprise you that I have problems with the extremists on both sides of the abortion issue. I find the extreme emphasis on pro-choice—which champions the absolute right of a woman to do whatever she wishes with her body—to be extremely selfish. In fact, I would describe such women and their supporters as "pro-self" rather than "pro-choice." Indeed, such extremists seem to take actual delight in ignoring others who should have a compelling interest in their choice, such as the father—and certainly the fetus whose developing life will be terminated. These extremists also often de-emphasize or even ignore contraception that would make abortion unnecessary. It is this blind focus on the "right to abortion" that I find morally offensive and medically inappropriate.

However, I find many anti-abortion extremists also to be morally offensive and intellectually shallow. Put bluntly, those who label abortion as "murder" too often ignore the many other forms of killing in our world in which the lives of innocent children and adults are snuffed out in war, in famine, and in social injustices of many kinds. Why don't anti-abortionists, these so-called pro-life people, focus equal energy on the slaughter of lives already born? Why don't they fight for the rights of the already born to have lives of full humanity? After all, there is a fate worse than death, often aptly described as a "living hell." So why don't pro-lifers fight for the social and financial resources to adequately take care of the lives they try to rescue from the womb? It seems to me that "pro-lifers" are all too often simply "pro-birthers." And when these advocates do not also support health and educational programs for the children who are born into this world (and the taxes to pay for them if they want the government to provide them), then they should be exposed for the narrowly focused hypocrites they are.

Indeed, I find so much hypocrisy on both sides of the abortion issue that I have become convinced that the extremists of both sides have become more interested in winning the battle against each other than in winning the war for full human life.

Well, Chick, I am sure this is enough to get you going. Your turn.

Sincerely,
Tim

Dear Tim,

I was surprised that you began discussing abortion as a *medical* issue. Almost no abortions are performed for medical indications; it is expedience that takes most women to the abortionist. I don't think I ever thought of abortion as a medical issue except, perhaps, from a regulatory point of view. For when any medical procedure is performed over one million times a year, some authority has to set the guidelines and make it safe. But abortion is a strange "medical procedure" because when a pregnant woman decides that she wants an abortion, she is not deciding anything about her health except in rare circumstances.

When you say that a woman wants to get rid of something in her body that she has decided will do her more harm than good, you trivialize the abortion issue. That has been the ploy of the pro-abortionists who would like to see abortion taken very lightly as a minor medical issue. That is more than "something" in her body. It is not, as they say, "a few membranes in the uterus." I've never yet asked a woman why she wanted an abortion without getting the answer: "I don't want a baby." She knows what it is: a *baby*. So should society.

When the abortion debate heated up about twenty-five years ago, it was primarily social activists and politicians who decided that women should not be "forced" to undergo an unwanted pregnancy, that a woman has the "right to her own body," and that her pregnant plight came about because this is a "chauvinistic" world. Abortion became a medical issue only because it happened to be doctors who became the executioners of the developing baby. What a travesty for a *life-saving* profession! When I was a medical student, an abortionist was viewed by the medical profession with a loathing usually reserved for some slimy crawly thing that came out from under an overturned rock.

I do agree with you, Tim, about the futility of the shrill cries from both sides, from those who are "pro-choice" *and* those who are "pro-life." The rhetoric has reached unprecedented heights, and the headlines in the newspapers remind me of World War II with "battle cry," "combat," "war," "battle strategy," and so on. Crushing the enemy has become the goal, to be achieved no matter what ethical and moral principles get trampled in the process. Success amounts to who can rent the largest number of school buses to transport marchers to Washington, D.C., for a demonstration. So, Tim, I think that abortion is *not* primarily a medical issue, but has become the largest social and political issue to divide our nation since slavery.

Sincerely,
Chick

Dear Chick,

I agree about the social and political part. In fact, I am terrified of the political consequences of the current battle. I believe the abortion issue has the potential to rip our society apart at the seams and to capture our political system as a hostage to the emotions of extremists. For example, there are increasing numbers of people who vote for a candidate only on the basis of his or her abortion stance, a view so narrow that it may not allow this country to survive its many other challenges. Having said that, I do think these extremists are out of step with most Americans. I believe that ultimately most Americans will value our tradition of free choice more strongly than their passions about abortion.

In fact, I am more concerned about nine individuals in Washington than I am about the collective wisdom of the American people. The Supreme Court has already begun to limit *Roe v. Wade*, the 1973 Supreme Court decision that made abortion legal. As that happens, Chick, I believe we will see a period of political chaos in which all the states will come up with their own version of an abortion law, leaving us with fifty different laws. That will promote migrations across state lines of the kind I saw in New York State when I was a hospital resident in the early 1970s. When that state became the first to liberalize its abortion laws, women immediately came from all over the country to take advantage of that law, and New York hospitals had to quickly put a cap on beds designated for abortions.

Speaking of New York, I recall a Catholic woman who was a leader in the anti-abortion movement in our community before the New York law changed. Despite her public posture, she privately arranged for a member of her family to fly to Sweden for an abortion, a graphic example of the discrimination according to wealth that will always exist in the absence of legal and financially available abortions. There is no doubt that when abortions are illegal, poor women experience discrimination; the poor go to back-alley abortionists and the rich fly to a country or state where abortions are legal. However, I also believe that the numbers of actual deaths from the days of back-alley abortions are sometimes conveniently overstated by pro-choice advocates; discrimination is wrong in its own right and we need not inflate numbers to argue the case.

In fact, it is mostly because of my concern about potential discrimination against the poor that I find myself saying that I am anti-abortion but also pro-choice. I do find the idea and act of abortion distasteful or even offensive. And I recognize that it definitely destroys a life in the making. But in our sinful world with less-than-perfect choices, I must support the right of each woman to decide what is the right choice for her and her family situation on this and so many other issues. I would champion the right of anyone, including extremists, to try and persuade others to their viewpoint. But I stop short of advocating laws that would restrict choice. In short, I am morally opposed to abortion but also philosophically opposed to government restriction of free choice and the inevitable discrimination that results.

And knowing you as I do, Chick, I suspect you are poised to pounce on that position.

Sincerely,
Tim

Dear Tim,

When you say that you are pro-choice but against abortion, you sound schizophrenic. The reason you want it both ways is that you don't let your concept of the sanctity of human life go back as far as it should. Tim, I know you wouldn't kill a *newborn* baby simply because its mother didn't want it. How, then, could you condone taking the life of an *unborn* baby?

Tim, I really don't think you are pro-choice. You are pro-abortion. Let's not let words and semantics cloud the issue. How can you say you are morally opposed to abortion, but philosophically opposed to government restriction of free choice? I imagine you are morally opposed to stealing, but would you endorse shoplifting under some circumstances? If you're pro-life, you're pro-life. Life is life.

Now let me respond to your political and social concerns. First, when you say that the number of illegal deaths from abortion were sometimes conveniently *over*stated, I think you really don't know how much. In the early 1970s, before *Roe v. Wade*, the pro-abortionists deliberately exaggerated the number of deaths from abortion. Even I believed what I read in the papers:

more than 10,000 abortion deaths a year. In truth,
fewer than 500 women died in any year from illegal
abortions. Obviously those deaths were tragic, but 500
a year is a long way from 10,000. And I think that one
of the most reprehensible things those now-confessed
liars ever did was to submit that kind of false evidence
before the Supreme Court.

You said you are concerned about discrimination.
I've always hated unfairness, and these days I spend a
lot of my time on the lecture circuit saying that
Americans suffer not only from diseases of the body
but also from diseases of society, of which poverty is
number one. But I have to admit, when the poor cannot
get abortions, I am relieved that unborn lives are saved
even though I remain distressed about unfairness.
However, if abortion is legal, as much as I despise it, it
should be legal for everybody in the same way.
(Speaking of unfairness, isn't it strange, Tim, that
people are more concerned about providing abortions
for the poor than for providing *life-saving* liver trans-
plants for the poor?)

Finally, on the issue of political extremism, let me
recall to your memory something most people don't
even consider: that if the anti-abortionists and the pro-
abortionists had sat down to talk it over before *Roe
v. Wade*, the pro-abortionists may well have been
content with a law allowing limited abortion only to
save the life of the mother, and for rape, incest, and a
severely handicapped fetus. Had that compromise, a
political one, been made, ninety-seven percent of the

abortions since 1973 would have been avoided. That never happened, because the anti-abortion people, in addition to being shrill, are also all-or-nothing people: "Give me everything I want or don't give me anything." And that's exactly what they got: nothing.

But, enough on the political and social aspects of abortion. I think you need to take on the real issue: the morality of abortion.

Sincerely,
Chick

Dear Chick,

First, I must say how surprised I am—and pained—at your oversimplification of my position, your need to see me as black-and-white on this issue. How could anyone except the extremist pro-choice person whom I described in my initial letter be "pro-abortion"? Just because I am not totally anti-abortion does not make me "pro-abortion"! I believe that abortion is a terrible tragedy, an awful solution to the problem of unwanted pregnancy; I would love to see a world in which abortion is not even known, let alone a popular option. But I also believe that in our sinful world—which too often puts human life at all stages in jeopardy—abortion is sometimes the best of appalling alternatives. In that sense I *am* pro-choice, as well as in the philosophical sense of believing that I do not have the right to impose my position about abortion on others and particularly not on the woman who has to live with the consequences of her choice in a way no one else ever can. In that regard, I am also troubled by the fact that most of the legal decisions about abortion are made by men who never have to live with the consequences of *their* decisions.

Now, what about the morality of abortion, which, as you say, is ultimately the "real issue"? There is no question that an abortion terminates a developing life. I use the word "developing" to indicate the distinction between a life not yet capable of existence *outside the womb* and one that is. And while both types of life are of value, I am one who believes that we should be more concerned about life *after birth*. I also believe that in a less than perfect world we are forced to make choices among less-than-perfect alternatives. And I believe there are situations in which it is morally appropriate to choose an abortion rather than bring into full existence a life condemned to pain and suffering and rejection.

Unfortunately, the Bible says nothing directly about abortion, does not even use the word! However, I would agree that the Old Testament does speak "protectively" in several passages about life in the womb. And yet, I find it especially instructive to note that Jesus does not even come close to discussing abortion, even though it was a common practice in his time. How could it be that one who was so willing to speak out on so many social conditions did not speak at all on this one, unless to indicate that it was not a matter of paramount importance to him?

This is also a logical time to face the issue of "the beginning of life." It is my impression, Chick, that many people hinge their position on abortion on their view of the beginning of life. Specifically, many take an anti-abortion position because they believe that life begins at conception and that abortion therefore destroys life. I agree that life is destroyed. But I think that such a narrow focus on the moment of conception blinds us to other important considerations.

My own view of the biology of human life is that life is a continuum from the sperm and egg as products of living persons, continuing in new form with conception, and entering still another stage when the fetus is capable of life outside the womb. And like many, I make an *emotional* if not *logical* distinction between life capable of existing on its own outside the womb versus fetal life before that point. Therefore I think all the debate about when "life" biologically begins diverts us from important decisions about life before and after the actual moment of conception.

For example, too much of our focus on preventing abortion occurs *after* conception, rather than thinking about preventing abortion by focusing more on contraception. Similarly, the focus on conception and life in the womb seems to blind so many anti-abortionists to the "slow dying" of so many of the "already living" in our world: the starving children and adults in so many countries, the innocent victims of war, the poor in our own urban neighborhoods. In fact, Chick, I have come to believe that much of the motivation of extreme anti-abortionists who so conveniently ignore these other problems has to do with their disgust with sexual pleasure or sex without procreation. For them, making abortion unavailable becomes a way of punishing what they regard as immoral or inappropriate sex.

So ultimately, Chick, when it comes to the morality of abortion, I must first examine my own thinking, then respect the right of others to do the same. Finally I must rest in the comfort of believing that God loves us all, saints and sinners alike.

Sincerely,
Tim

Dear Tim,

I disagree with you on the "beginning of life" issue because I don't see life as a continuum from one generation to another. Rather, I see it as a continuum from conception to death. I believe that each human life has a definite beginning and that that beginning is conception.

You need to draw the line somewhere, and I think that conception is the only logical place. I say this because when the twenty-three chromosomes from the sperm and the twenty-three chromosomes from the egg unite at conception into one cell, that cell contains the forty-six chromosomes for the entire genetic code of a full human being, for a "me" or for a "you." That cell starts the process of life and growth: one cell, then two cells, then four, then eight, then sixteen, and so on through the stages the biologists call an embryo, fetus, newborn, baby, child, adolescent, adult. *It is all there from the beginning.* A tiny embryo has a beating heart, fingerprints, and electrical activity in its brain. Biologists have no argument that life begins at conception if they are talking about doves, chimpanzees, or horses. It is only when they are talking about the highest form of life—human beings—that philosophy supersedes biologic fact.

The "beginning of life" argument is important because there is a large segment of the population that says emphatically: "If I *knew* that life began at conception, I would have to be opposed to abortion." That always made sense to me. I believe that life begins at conception, that abortion takes a human life, and that therefore abortion is immoral.

I really don't see how you can say the debate over when "life begins" is biologically unnecessary and diverts us from the "important decisions," especially if you say that life is a continuum. If you are willing to eliminate the first stage in that continuum—the embryo—or even the second stage: the fetus—might you be willing to eliminate the next stage—a newborn baby? I don't think you would. So, Tim, if you would be unwilling to take the life of a newborn infant, why would you not oppose its life being snuffed out a minute before birth, or a minute before that, or a minute before that, and so on, all the way back to conception?

Tim, my concern for the unborn does not in any way alter my concern for, as you call it, the "slow dying" of so many of the already-born in our world. These days I spend much more time speaking and writing about the welfare of the living than of the unborn, and I am disturbed, as you are, that some anti-abortion people seem to wear blinders to keep them from seeing so many of this world's suffering people.

Although abortion is not mentioned in the Bible, there are passages that speak more than "protectively" of the fetus; these passages refer to actual purpose in the life of the fetus. In Psalm 139 David writes about God's role in his own life before birth:

> For you created my inmost being;
> you knit me together in my mother's womb.
> I praise you because I am fearfully and
> wonderfully made . . .
> your eyes saw my unformed body.
> All the days ordained for me
> were written in your book
> before one of them came to be.

When God called Jeremiah to be a prophet, we see reference to prenatal purpose in Jeremiah 1:5:

> Before I formed you in the womb I knew (chose) you,
> before you were born I set you apart;
> I appointed you as a prophet to the nations.

And I think you are taking great liberties in trying to decide what Jesus was thinking when he didn't talk about abortion. He didn't talk about slavery either.

Finally, I didn't mean to level a "painful charge" against you. What I meant to express is that I am so anti-abortion—based on my reverence for the *sanctity* of human life—that abortion is simply not in my armamentarium of advice. I feel that so strongly, and you feel the opposite. And I say that, Tim, knowing that you too are truly anti-abortion in the best of all possible worlds.

Your friend, as always,
Chick

Dear Chick,

I knew that we would remain friends through this dialogue, but thanks for putting it in writing. As you say, I would be anti-abortion in the best of all possible worlds. But the human sinfulness and selfishness that has created such terrible suffering and poverty in our world means that this is *not* the best of all possible worlds. And I have very reluctantly concluded that there are circumstances in which abortion may be the "best" of a list of very bad choices. I know that you cannot agree with that position, but at least you can apparently understand that being reluctantly pro-choice does not make me "pro" abortion. In short, it would seem that we agree on our "moral" opposition to abortion. What we can't harmonize is our willingness to allow others to make choices with which we might disagree. That will probably always be the space in which we will "agree to disagree."

Believe it or not, I can understand (though I disagree with it) your position on the poor not having access to abortions—i.e., your being "relieved that unborn lives are saved even though I am distressed about unfairness." At least you are brutally consistent. And you carry that consistency through to what must be a bitter end for you by saying that if abortion is legal, it should be legal for everyone in the same way.

I would also again point out that I make an important distinction between the time period when life is capable of existence outside the womb and before that time. Therefore I oppose fetal life being "snuffed out" a minute before birth, but I find the termination of fetal life before the time it is capable of independent life outside the womb more tolerable.

Now, how do we get on the road that we both want to travel: reducing the growing number of abortions in our world? Short of trying to eliminate abortions by legal fiat there are, I think, some realistic alternatives that need to be emphasized, namely, adoption and contraception. I do believe we could do a much better job of providing adoption care for pregnant women who do not want their babies but would be willing with proper support to make them available to couples so desperately wanting children. However, because the real problem leading to abortion is unwanted pregnancy, the best answer to abortion is contraception.

In fact, I am amazed that so many opponents of

abortion are so lukewarm or even negative about contraception. Some opposition to contraception, of course, comes from religious conviction. But much of it comes either from stupidity or apathy, or political fear of the far right. I think that it is time for the leaders in the anti-abortion movement to become strongly pro-contraception, albeit within the boundaries of their religious or moral conviction. And I would like very much to hear your thoughts about contraception in general, and specifically about the opposition to contraception of the religious far right and the Catholic church.

Sincerely,
Tim

Dear Tim,

Okay. We can agree that we are both morally opposed to abortion. And although I think you let the pro-abortion people hide too easily behind the "pro-choice" label, you remind me that decent and thoughtful people make a distinction between life before birth and life after birth. You are decent and thoughtful, and you make that distinction. I don't, and I think that people rarely change sides on this issue.

We also agree that the decision to have an abortion—or not to have an abortion—can be agonizing, painful, and carry lifelong consequences. And this kind of situation is usually made more agonizing because either abortion or birth was a difficult solution to a problem that could have been avoided. Abortion is not really the problem—the problem is unwanted pregnancy. The best way to eliminate abortion is to eliminate unwanted pregnancies. And to eliminate unwanted pregnancies, women and men, especially young people, must be instructed in ways to prevent those pregnancies. That means contraception.

Our society knows pitifully little about contraception and birth control. I believe that Americans often confuse contraception and birth control. All contraception is birth control, but not all birth control is contraception. Anything that stops births from occurring is birth control: abstinence, contraception, abortion, even war and famine. Some methods of birth control are abortifacient: They destroy the fertilized egg or make it impossible for it to find a place of nurture in the womb. They abort the pregnancy that would otherwise have continued until birth. Contraception, however, avoids birth by avoiding conception, by keeping the sperm from fertilizing the egg.

I think that America is ripe for a campaign to promote understanding of birth control and contraception. Of course there are barriers, the largest one being the Roman Catholic church. It seems to me that Catholics are placed in an almost impossible situation. Their church opposes abortion (correctly, I think), but then also opposes contraception, the most likely way to avoid abortions.

Of course, many Catholics simply ignore the

church's teaching on this point, as one recent poll reported that seventy percent of Roman Catholics are practicing contraception, while thirty percent of priests approve of it. But the Roman Catholic church seems to wield an influence that extends beyond its own constituents. I discovered this when I discussed with Catholic authorities the issue of condom use, not for contraception but for AIDS prevention. They didn't budge and made clear their opposition to condom use for disease prevention even by non-Catholics. I believe that this Catholic opposition is a major factor in keeping us from pursuing the contraception education programs that Americans so clearly need. And I think that this reluctance to deal with contraception has stalled much-needed research in contraception.

Every abortion is the result of failure, a failure to practice contraception, a failure to practice contraception correctly, a failure of our institutions whether family, economic, or social. I imagine that even the most rabid pro-abortionists do not want abortions to happen. Both sides of the abortion war should agree that abortions are tragic failures. And, for the most part, they are preventable failures.

In response to a continuing flood of invitations to speak to various groups all across the country, I have said that I will speak to neither side of the abortion issue until they start talking to each other. It can happen quietly, without fanfare. In any community the anti-abortion groups and abortion-rights activists—while agreeing to disagree on the right to an abortion—

could cooperate, could work together to reduce the number of unwanted pregnancies. That is a way out of the abortion stalemate that both sides could support.

Sincerely,
Chick

P.S. I, too, lament the opportunities missed in adoption. The emotional distress of couples unable to have children is a serious social and, at times, medical problem. Adoption would serve the unwilling mother-to-be as well as the parent couple.

*

There is a time for everything . . .
a time to be born and a time to die. . . .
ECCLESIASTES 3:1, 2

2
Euthanasia

Dear Chick,

Now that we've sparred on abortion, we should take on the other "life and death" issue of our time: euthanasia. As you know, the most literal translation of the word "euthanasia" would be "a good death." So who could be against that, except an extremist who would argue that terminal suffering should be accepted, unchanged by human intervention, as "fate" or "God's will"? I personally believe that helping someone die in peace and without pain, even if that might hasten the biological timetable of death by a few hours or even days, is not only acceptable but is mandatory for modern medical care. Unfortunately, as we both know, too many physicians are still either ignorant about good pain control, or inappropriately afraid of addicting a terminal patient to medication.

But providing modern pain control is not the issue that has aroused our society and the medical profession. At stake in the current discussion about "euthanasia" are actions that go beyond providing pain control to the actual withdrawal of so-called life-support measures, or, far more controversial, providing the knowledge and tools for a person to actually take his or her own life—in short, to commit suicide. These activities, often referred to as "mercy killing," do take us to the edge of both ethical and theological debate. Indeed, I would argue that our views of life and God will have a profound impact on our views of such activities.

Specifically, if one believes that "life" is no more than earthly "physical existence," then it would be somewhat logical to prolong such life at all cost. But if one believes that our earthly lives are only part of the continuing stream of our existence, then the frantic prolongation of earthly life may be nothing more than "biological idolatry"—worship at the altar of physical existence. (I am reminded of a comment reportedly made at a meeting of the visiting committee of the Harvard Medical School, that one way to reduce health-care costs would be to restore belief in life after death.)

Similarly, if we view God as a celestial terminator determining precisely the time and manner of each human death, then we might be reluctant to interfere with God's apparent timetable for a human life. But in fact, we interfere with that apparent timetable all the time by using modern medical tools to routinely prevent what would otherwise be certain death. And we often do so explicitly in the belief that God has given us these tools precisely for that purpose!

So if we believe that life is more than earthly existence and that God's control of the universe does not preclude using modern medical tools to interfere with the "course of nature," then does not logic at least allow us to consider such activities as withdrawing life-support or providing for a biologically premature death that avoids unnecessary physical and/or emotional suffering? At this point, Chick, I will try to be more precise.

First, the so-called withdrawal of life-support. I use the phrase, "so-called" because I believe that we all too often fail to distinguish between "life-support" and "death-support." In my judgment, no one should want to withdraw measures that offer hope of restoration to some kind of meaningful human existence, which I would define as the ability to interact in some meaningful way with fellow human beings. But we increasingly find ourselves in the bind of having used available medical technology to prolong the act of dying rather than salvaging the chance for meaningful life. As we both well know, it is often impossible to initially tell which pathway we are choosing. My own view would be that whenever there is a reasonable doubt, we should err on the side of possible life. But all too often when there is very good evidence that meaningful life will never again be possible, the act of dying is prolonged more to ease the family's guilt (or fear of legal consequences) rather than to do what's best for the patient. I am reminded of an observation written by Rabbi Joseph Edelheit about the well-known Scripture in Deuteronomy 30:19: "I have set before you life and death, the blessings and curses. Now choose life, so that you . . . may live." Says the Rabbi, "Were Moses speaking today, I pray he would charge us with a more relevant admonition: 'Choose life . . . unless it is a machine.'"

In fact, most of us are quite willing to consider so-called *passive* euthanasia: withdrawing life-support measures in situations where a patient is clearly in the final terminal stages and it is the act of dying which is being prolonged. But what about the much more controversial act of assisting in the termination of a life marked by conscious awareness and not yet in the final stage of death? Put simply, while I personally gag at the idea of helping a person to commit suicide, I am at least willing to theoretically consider the possibility under very limited circumstances. I say this because I have always believed that a physician has a dual role: to preserve life *and* prevent suffering. And, I believe, that both are equally valid and sometimes in conflict. Let me emphasize that I am willing to consider physician-assisted suicide *only in situations of clearly terminal illness in which there is no hope of ultimate recovery*.

As I have said, in such situations I believe we have a paramount duty to keep the person free of physical pain, and that we have the tools to do so. But what if the pain is primarily psychic? What if the patient suffers most from a fear of losing control in the final stages of death, of becoming a burden to family and society, of having to live a conscious but totally unacceptable (to him/her) life of physical or mental incompetence? Is there any reason we should consider aiding such people to commit suicide if they are determined to do so?

As you know, this matter was brought to a more controversial focus by the actions of a Rochester, New York internist, Dr. Timothy Quill. He described in the *New England Journal of Medicine* (April 7, 1991) his decision to prescribe enough barbiturates for a terminal leukemia patient to be able to commit suicide at the time of her choice. As he states in his article, "I had an uneasy feeling about the boundaries I was exploring— spiritual, legal, professional and personal. Yet I also felt strongly that I was setting her free to get the most out of the time she had left, and to maintain dignity and control on her own terms until her death." I find it much harder to dismiss the careful and thoughtful action of Dr. Quill than, for example, the reckless action of a doctor who helps an Alzheimer's patient whom he hardly knows commit suicide in the back of his van. But even when done with dignity and thought-fulness, ultimately the issue for a doctor still comes down to this: Is it ever justified to help end a life that is still conscious and reasonably free from physical pain?

My own very personal answer is to say no, but reluctantly. I say "reluctantly" because I sympathize with people who feel they have no control over their dying, that the medical and legal professions have arrogantly obliterated their control over the "right to die with dignity." But I think the *legalized* participation of physicians in the suicide of their patients is fraught with too many moral and practical dangers that outweigh its possible benefit. Those dangers include inappropriate pressure to terminate life for financial, family, or societal reasons that are not consonant with the best interests of the person, and a potential poisoning of the trust between patient and doctor that is ultimately too precious to place at risk.

Having indicated my own personal position—and my own opposition to legalizing physician-assisted suicide—I will stop short of condemning other physicians who may come to different conclusions. In the Netherlands, the "solution" to this issue has been to continue the law that makes physician-assisted suicide illegal, but to informally "allow" such activity according to strict guidelines structured by the Royal Dutch Society for the Promotion of Medicine (KNMG). That may be a reasonable societal compromise that allows individual physicians to act in a responsible fashion without fear of prosecution, while keeping legal pressure against inappropriate suicide assistance.

In short, I have once again come to a position where I state my own personal decision on this issue but am unwilling to impose that position legally on others. Your turn!

Sincerely,
Tim

Dear Tim,

Once again, I think that you are too soft on people
who disagree with you on these vital life-and-death
issues. I agree with your position that you would not
help to end a life "that is still conscious and free from
physical pain," but I do not come to that decision
reluctantly as you do. And, unlike you, I am not at all
reluctant to denounce other physicians who disagree
with me on this issue. I believe that the Hippocratic
oath has kept physicians on the right course for two
thousand years and that we should not abandon the
Hippocratic teaching affirming that physicians will
never be involved in killing their patients: "Others who
call themselves physicians may suggest and do these
things, but as for us, we are above such things and can
be trusted to do no harm."

You and I also differ on the Dutch stance. You
mentioned the Netherlands and its current trend
toward euthanasia. During the Second World War I
was proud of my Dutch ancestry when Dutch physicians chose to be shot in the village square rather than
take part in Nazi euthanasia experiments. I am amazed
and ashamed that today a growing number of patients
in Dutch hospitals die by a lethal injection given by
their physicians.

In all discussions about euthanasia, Tim, I think
that the slippery slope argument is a compelling one. I
don't think you see the dangers of the slippery slope. I

am convinced that in the 1930s the German medical sentiment favoring euthanasia (even before Hitler came to power) made it easier for the Nazi government to move society along the slippery slope that led to the Holocaust. The German euthanasia movement started with defective babies, then reached out to eliminate the insane, then to those suffering from senile dementia, then to patients with advanced tuberculosis, to amputees deemed of no further service to the Reich, to gypsies, to Poles, and finally to Jews. The Holocaust was upon us. And when abortion became legal throughout America, I frequently said that widespread abortion would have the effect of cheapening our view of life, so that infanticide (the killing of defective newborns) and then euthanasia would soon be tolerated, then sanctioned, then made legal. At first people said we would never have this kind of slippery slope, but I'm afraid that I've been proven right.

Tim, having fired back at you this way, let me say that I quote you frequently on the lecture circuit, when I pass along your perceptive observation that there has always been an element of tension or paradox in our view of life as understood in our Judeo-Christian heritage. We cherish life and do all we can to sustain it, but our spiritual heritage reminds us that we should not equate being *terminally* ill with being *hopelessly* ill. As for me, my Christian faith allows me to face death with realism and even optimism.

In any discussion of euthanasia I think we have to be very careful in defining what it means to help someone die "without pain." That could be interpreted as helping them by killing them; or actually helping them to commit suicide by providing them with the knowledge to commit suicide; or of standing back at an appropriate time and letting nature take its course while making the comfort of the patient of highest priority. Of that list of possibilities, I could do only the last . . . and have done it in my surgical practice.

Perhaps, Tim, I should stop talking philosophy for a minute and describe a real-life situation that I had to face all too often when I was a pediatric surgeon. Let's imagine, Tim, that you had a three-year-old little girl with an abdominal tumor, a neuroblastoma. I operated on your little girl, and after surgery it was appropriate to treat her with both radiation therapy and chemotherapy. Even though she has improved for a while, she still has a malignant tumor. You have brought her to see me, and on this office visit I notice that she has been failing, and I think you have seen the downward trend, too, so I am going to sit down and chat with you about what I think we should do from now on. Here's what I would say (in ordinary practice I might take an hour to say what I'm going to write you in the next paragraph):

"Tim, I'm sure you can see that your little girl is failing, and I want you to know where we stand. I've done all the surgery that I can do. Further radiation and chemotherapy seem to me to be futile because of the spread of her tumor in spite of those methods of therapy. In fact, I am going to suggest that we discontinue the chemotherapy. Let me tell you why. On the one hand, if we discontinue treatment and do nothing for your little girl, I think that she will probably succumb to her tumor in about six weeks, but she will be without pain and without suffering. On the other hand, if we treat her with chemotherapy, on the basis of my past experience with similar problems, I would predict that she could live about three months, but before she died she would be in pain and might be blind and deaf because of the treatment. So, Tim, I recommend that we stand back and let nature take its course."

I don't think that's euthanasia; I think it's good medicine. I think it's good medicine for the child, for the family, for all of us.

I think we're on the same wavelength when you distinguish between "life support" and "death support," although I would probably call it "dying support." I also agree that, when in doubt, *err on the side of life*. With that in mind, my unwavering faith in God and his plan for our lives is a basic tenet of my faith and the way I live and practice medicine. God gave us the ability to invent an aspirin tablet as well as to invent life-support systems such as respirators. These skills, I believe, have been given to be held in stewardship. When I am dealing with a patient, I feel that I have a primary responsibility to him or her, then a responsibility to the patient's family, but ultimately my responsibility is to God for the manner in which I use the gifts he has given me to deal with the lives of my patients.

I am concerned about a new tendency to interpret suffering too loosely. When medical students ask me why I went into medicine, I tell them unhesitatingly, "in order to save lives and alleviate suffering." And it was my patient's life that I tried to save, it was my patient's suffering that I tried to alleviate. Today, however, when a patient is terminally ill and the family is suffering, some people say the patient's life should be terminated in order to alleviate the suffering of the family. This perverted sentiment has no place in the practice of medicine.

But then, Tim, you raise the question of keeping a person free of pain when that pain is primarily psychic. And you seem to accept the actions of the doctor in New York who prescribed barbiturates for a leukemia patient who did not wish to continue therapy or life. I think that physician's actions were reprehensible. As we both know, by his own admission he began discussing suicide with his patient many months before he assisted her suicide. This was not a patient dying with intractable pain. Her cancer, for which therapy offered at least a twenty-five percent chance of remission, may have led her to view the future with great uncertainty, to feel a loss of personal control in her life, to feel unable to face the ups and downs of her situation. But those feelings, common as they are to well and sick people alike, are completely insufficient reason for a physician to abandon his or her sacred role of the healer and instead to become a killer. I believe that the New York doctor who prescribed the barbiturates should have spent those months building his patient's determination to fight on, not to prepare her for suicide. As Margaret Mead once said, "We have come full circle from the pre-Hippocratic days. Once again, the patient does not know whether the approaching physician is coming in the guise of healer or killer." How sad.

I am also saddened and alarmed by the growing demands that nutrition and fluids be classified as "treatment" just so they can be withdrawn from a patient in the guise of stopping "futile treatment." I think that amounts to death by starvation and dehydration, and it should be condemned. What do you think?

Sincerely,
Chick

Dear Chick,

Obviously there is much we can agree upon in this matter right off the bat. Indeed, as I read your letter, the only real issue for further discussion between us is whether or not physicians should give potentially lethal medicines, either directly or by prescription, for reasons other than complete pain control—i.e., for such reasons as psychic pain or fear of loss of control in the face of a clearly terminal illness. You condemn all physicians who engage in "assisted suicide." I am reluctant to condemn them all because I feel that some are acting in good faith, trying to relieve suffering according to careful guidelines and only in situations of illnesses that are clearly destined to be terminal.

For example, I would not characterize Dr. Quill's actions as "reprehensible" as you do, though they were certainly provocative. I also think you are being far too harsh on Dutch physicians by being "totally ashamed" of their actions. Indeed, I applaud the Royal Dutch Society for the Promotion of Medicine for attempting to develop careful guidelines regarding when it *might* be appropriate for physicians to aid in the suicide of their patients. By using the word "might" I mean to indicate that like the Dutch, I strongly believe we should never make physician-assisted suicide a "duty" of physicians or a "right" to be expected by patients. But I do believe we should "allow" individual physicians and patients to come to mutual understanding on this matter without fear of inappropriate legal harassment. And speaking of abuse, the latest data on the Dutch experience would indicate that at least so far, the Dutch climate has not led to an explosion of such activity. For example, one study (*Lancet*) indicates that only about three percent of all deaths in Holland are caused by doctors who actually directly help patients to end their own lives, either via injections or giving patients enough medication to commit suicide.

Having indicated my willingness to allow others to consider assisted suicide, I believe it is time to also champion an alternative to suicide—namely, so-called comfort care, best known in its hospice form. We should be doing far more in our health-care system to develop and support local hospices. If hospices were geographically and financially available, I believe that the person considering suicide would prefer the hospice. In fact, if we did an adequate job of providing such care, the issue of physician-assisted suicide would largely disappear.

I share your worries about legalized assisted suicide. For example, I worry about what the easy availability of legalized physician-assisted suicide would do to family dynamics. It might force every terminally ill person and his or her family to consider the possibility that would, in turn, create financial and social pressures to take the quicker way out.

I am also worried that if physician-assisted suicide were legalized, the disenfranchised in our society—the poor and handicapped and abandoned—could easily be denied adequate terminal care. Put bluntly, who would be around to defend *their* rights? I also worry, as you do, about the impact of readily available assisted suicide on physician-patient relationships. Patients could easily come to wonder about the commitment of their physicians to the often difficult care in terminal illness. And physicians, being human, could be tempted to take the quick way, or to put subtle pressure on patients and their families to do so.

These kinds of considerations—these slippery slopes—ultimately force me to take a stand against the legalization of physician-assisted suicide. However, I would favor a pathway similar to that of the Netherlands where assisted suicide is "allowed" according to very careful guidelines, but not made legal. I do not want to open the legal gates to make such activity easy or routine. And the ultimate authority for decision making about care during terminal illness should lie with the patient, not with the medical profession or society. But I also believe that society should maintain safeguards to make sure that patients are protected from family members or physicians who would take advantage of legalized physician-assisted suicide.

Finally, a reaction to your opposition to withdrawing food and fluids: I am not opposed to such withdrawal in certain circumstances, namely those circumstances in which they, too, along with breathing support, have become an artificial means of prolonging death rather than life. I recognize that we have special emotional attachments to the providing of food and water. But if we can keep the patient comfortable during the withdrawal phase, I think that food and water should be included on the list of "support" measures that can artificially prolong death rather than support meaningful life. Time for your reactions.

Sincerely,
Tim

Dear Tim,

When you say that Dutch or American physicians are acting in "good faith" when they participate in physician-assisted suicide, what does that mean? When the Mafia puts out a contract on a victim, the killer acts in good faith. The question is not one of good faith but whether we as a society stand ready to countenance the legalized killing of one person by another. A doctor cannot be both healer and killer.

And by the way, Tim, I take no comfort when you say that in the Netherlands "only" three percent of the deaths in that country are directly caused by doctors. In the United States, that would amount to *only* 64,860 killings by doctors per year!

Furthermore, as more is learned about the Netherlands experience, it seems those Dutch statistics cannot be trusted. As euthanasia becomes more commonplace, it is reported less accurately and less frequently.

I am concerned about the role that "depression" seems to play in so many of these patient-suicide cases. If emotional depression ever becomes an approved reason for physician-assisted suicide, then the practice of medicine—and many patients—will be in real jeopardy. Can you imagine what would happen in the practice of psychiatry? This issue of depression heightens my concern when a handbook on suicide becomes a bestseller. Depression is usually a temporary condition, certainly among the many adolescents who become depressed. It is already a national tragedy that suicide—usually depression-induced—has become the leading cause of death in female teenagers.

And even in the severely ill, depression can be only temporary. Do you remember the woman in California who wanted to die because she was paraplegic? She asked to be starved to death in the hospital, but the nurses refused. The press reports on this incident almost always focused on the suicide demands of the depressed patient, generally ignoring the larger story: Only a month before, she had been obviously enjoying life, she had just been offered a new and rewarding job, and she was about to be married. But then her fiancè left her, the job was withdrawn, so she became depressed and said that she wanted to die. When this case eventually found its way to the courts, the judge refused to order her death in the hospital, saying that if she wanted to commit suicide, she would have to do it at home. When the woman went home, she benefited from some support services and soon decided that life is indeed worth living. It's cases like this that make me so concerned when the reasons for advocating "good death" shift from intractable pain to dissatisfaction with what life holds. And I am very fearful about placing societal pressure or family pressure on terminally ill people to "hurry up and move out of the way."

I'm sure that you realize that in cases of severe pain where therapy is futile (as in the last weeks of some cancers), I would simply prescribe sedation and let nature take its course. But to allow physician-assisted suicide to terminate a life because of any one of a number of emotional issues is something that my faith and my view of medicine cannot approve. In this controversy as in the controversy about abortion, I can see clearly the two sides to each issue, but I cannot condone killing either the unborn or the dying.

Finally, Tim, in regard to selective euthanasia, we must be concerned with what the next step is likely to be. Societies always tend to expand the number of conditions and groups targeted for this "special treatment" or "final solution," and I agree with the concerns you express about the impact of medically sanctioned suicide on the poor and handicapped members of our society. I don't think that there are *any* legitimate circumstances in which a physician should consider assisting in the suicide of a patient. I remain true to the stand I took with the Hippocratic oath: to try to be a healer but *never* a killer.

Sincerely,
Chick

Dear Chick,

I feel the need to respond briefly to your last letter, specifically to make clear again that I would be willing to consider physician-assisted suicide only in situations of clearly terminal illness with only a few weeks or months of life left. Your example of the California woman, for example, is a good one because it is precisely the kind of case I would *not* consider either for withdrawal or for more active assistance since it does not represent a terminal illness. But in someone who is clearly terminal—for example, a woman with ovarian cancer that has spread throughout the abdomen, or a man with prostate cancer spread throughout his bones—I could understand the mutual desire between patient and doctor to prevent the agony of the final descent into an unaided death. I would not personally be able to provide assistance, but I would want to make that possible for others without legal harassment.

As with abortion, I think that we have reached a point beyond which we cannot agree. So let's move to another subject, namely, AIDS. And I would like to suggest that we focus primarily on the social and ethical issues that swirl around this terrible disease.

Sincerely,
Tim

*

Do not judge,
and you will not be judged.
Do not condemn,
and you will not be condemned.
Forgive,
and you will be forgiven.

LUKE 6:37

3

AIDS

Dear Tim,

It seems hard to remember now, but when I was designated as Surgeon General I had never heard about AIDS, and even the handful of scientists who recognized it as an immunodeficiency problem didn't even know what to call it, much less what it really is. I'm sure that you remember reading the early reports, and I'm sure you realized as I did that we had a strange and dangerous disease on the loose. It started unremarkably when, in June 1981, the Centers for Disease Control reported that five "previously healthy" homosexuals were admitted to Los Angeles hospitals with a very rare form of pneumonia, *pneumocystis carinii*. Five cases are not many, but this lethal disease is so rare that a handful of cases in one place is striking. That small beginning led to the AIDS epidemic of the late 1980s. For a short time some people called it GRID—gay-related immune deficiency—but when cases showed up in nonhomosexuals, it was termed "acquired immune deficiency syndrome," and then just AIDS.

In the beginning, AIDS was less a medical issue than a political one. There were many facets to the politics of AIDS, but there was one enduring political conflict: AIDS pitted the politics of the homosexual revolution of the 1970s against the politics of the Reagan revolution of the 1980s. In the early years of AIDS—also the early years of the Reagan administration—health officials were astounded and dismayed by the link between the spread of AIDS and the promiscuity of some homosexual behavior: Many AIDS patients admitted to an astounding number of sexual encounters with an equally astounding number of different partners in a single day. Such revelations, along with the high incidence of rectal or anal intercourse (sodomy) led scientists to understand one method of AIDS transmission: from the semen of one person to the blood of the other. But there was a strong reluctance to discuss these sensitive (some said abhorrent) issues publicly, so, under directions from more than one White House source, health officials simply made vague references to "exchanging body fluids," thereby limiting considerably the public understanding of AIDS.

By the mid-1980s, even though much about AIDS

remained a mystery, we had learned a lot about the disease, much more than we learned in a similar time about many other diseases. We identified the virus and we now understood the spread of AIDS among homosexuals and IV-drug abusers. After identifying antibodies to the AIDS virus, researchers developed a screening test to make the blood supply safer for transfusion.

My own intense involvement with AIDS came after President Reagan finally asked me to write a report to the American people on AIDS. And then, two years later, because AIDS posed such a unique threat to the health of the American people, Congress took the unusual step of authorizing the Surgeon General to send a letter about what had become a dread disease to every household in the United States. For those two years AIDS took over my life.

They were difficult years, Tim, because the world around me seemed to turn upside down. At first I did not realize what an impact the Surgeon General's Report on AIDS had on the public. Suddenly I found myself praised by my former liberal adversaries and condemned by my former conservative allies. Of course, praise is always pleasant to accept, but the opposition troubled me, especially because it often came from people whom I considered my friends. I used to say that castigation by the *political* right, although disappointing and unpleasant did not unduly upset me; after all, castigation seemed to be their business. But I did feel a deep sense of betrayal by those on the *religious* right who took me to task. I have always felt that my position on AIDS was dictated by both scientific integrity and Christian compassion. I felt that my Christian opponents abandoned their own commitment to integrity and compassion.

My job as Surgeon General was to warn the American people about threats to their health. AIDS was a threat, and so my job was to treat AIDS, not as a political or social problem, but as a medical problem, a public-health problem. The job was simple: to save lives. I disapprove strongly of the forms of behavior responsible for most AIDS transmission: promiscuity, homosexual behavior, sex outside of marriage, and drug use. My Christian faith forms the basis for my moral standards, and I knew that the practice of homosexuality is anathema to most Christians, who see it as sinful. But as a physician it was my job to prolong lives and alleviate suffering. It was not my job to make decisions about treatment based upon how the disease or injury was incurred. As you know from your own experience, Tim, any doctor who has served her or his time in an emergency room knows that if two people arrive in an emergency room at the same time, both victims of wounds from their gun fight, one a police-man, one a robber, the doctor treats the most severely injured first, no matter what.

As Christians we are to treat those in need with compassion, just as Jesus did. Judgment is God's business. As Surgeon General, guided by Christian compassion and medical ethics, my course was clear: to do all I could to halt the spread of AIDS by educating the American people, accurately and completely.

To do that, I had to say things that I really would rather have not said. It was difficult for an old-timer of seventy, then about to celebrate his fiftieth wedding anniversary, to talk in public and before Congress about condoms. But I never mentioned the use of condoms as a preventive measure against AIDS without *first* stressing the much better and much safer alternatives of *abstinence* and *monogamy*. I also said that except for education, condoms were all we had to offer and that they were not one hundred percent reliable. Often I would spend several minutes of a speech extolling abstinence and monogamy (for social and moral reasons as well as reasons of health), and then at the end I would say that any persons who are foolish enough not to practice abstinence or mutually faithful monogamy should use a latex condom to protect themselves and their partner. Usually, the media would repeat only what I said about condoms. That annoyed me.

As you remember, Tim, many people acknowledged the need to have AIDS education, but then they became disturbed when they realized that would mean sex education as well. But I hoped that even people who normally opposed public-school sex education would see that we needed very explicit sex education because if kids are sexually active in the age of AIDS, they could die.

I saw a unique opportunity for religious groups

normally opposed to sex education to use the threat of AIDS to produce a morally-based sex education program that would conform to their moral standards and also serve to protect a generation of youngsters from AIDS. In Africa and Asia, AIDS is primarily a heterosexually transmitted disease and so will it be in the United States—eventually. But for now in the United States, most people who get AIDS are intravenous drug users and homosexuals. As far as preventing the spread of AIDS, science and traditional Christian morality stand in agreement: *Sexual behavior should be either abstinence or monogamy.*

But all too many people fell back on old fears and prejudice. And that is still the problem with AIDS. Although we will continue to hear about more and more people who have become infected with the HIV virus through heterosexual contact, nonetheless most Americans who get AIDS are intravenous drug users and homosexuals. And because the number of HIV-positive people among minority groups, especially blacks and Hispanics, is growing at an alarming and disproportionate rate, we are facing the same old problem: How, Tim, are we going to provide medical treatment fairly and compassionately to people who suffer from multiple forms of discrimination?

Sincerely,
Chick

Dear Chick,

I, too, remember vividly my first encounter with what was to become the AIDS epidemic. I had read the report on the five cases of very unusual pneumonias in gay men in Los Angeles and had decided to do a report on the subject on "Good Morning America." I felt that even this early report was so significant that we should offer a preliminary warning to the gay community about the possibility of a serious medical problem being spread through homosexual activity. It just so happened that a columnist for the *Boston Globe* chose that particular morning to "survey" the three network morning news programs and write a column about "morning television." And he made a rather sarcastic comment about my deciding to talk about "buggery" (sodomy) on morning television. (I subsequently wrote him a private letter saying that he had a right to his views about morning television but that I thought he was underestimating the particular importance of this new disease pattern, and to his credit he subsequently apologized in print several times for having made light of my subject.)

In fact, that episode was typical of many early responses to what became the AIDS crisis. It revealed a confused or cynical and sometimes downright prejudiced position that stemmed more from a focus on homosexuality than on a disease process that happened to be primarily found initially among gay men. And I have always felt that the gay community has a legiti-

mate point in saying that if AIDS had first been
discovered among white heterosexuals, it would have
received a lot more serious attention a lot more quickly.

Which brings me to the continuing issue of the
prejudice directed toward the gay community regarding AIDS and many other issues. I too agree that when
it comes to treating disease and disability, we must
always separate our feelings about the activity from our
concern about the person. But clearly, when it comes to
homosexuality, that is difficult for many people, especially for those who believe for religious reasons that
homosexuality is a sin.

That religious belief, of course, stems from biblical
passages in both the Old and New Testaments that
condemn homosexuality, sometimes quite strongly.
Those passages cannot be "wished away" but I would
make two observations that I think should minimize
anyone's rush to judgment against homosexuals on the
basis of "what the Bible says."

First, there are many other kinds of human behavior which the Bible condemns just as strongly—sometimes even more strongly—but which we conveniently
ignore. Even the passages that mention homosexuality
usually include it as one of many sins, most of which
we conveniently excuse because they hit too close to
home. Persons who make homosexuality a major focus
of their concern about sin are being very selective in
their emphasis. Some psychologists attribute that selec-
tivity (and the sometimes resultant homophobia) to a
certain degree of ambivalent feelings that most of us

have about our sexuality. Therefore we tend to fear that which we find threatening or upsetting. Clearly there are many sound medical reasons to condemn promiscuous homosexual activity of the kind you describe as well as promiscuous heterosexual activity. But we should recognize that when we become selectively focused on homosexuality, we are not responding biblically. I should also point out that Jesus says nothing about homosexuality but says a lot about compassion for the outcast in society.

The other reason for being careful about condemning homosexuals is the growing evidence for some kind of genetic influence among a certain segment of homosexuals, those who describe an attraction toward the same sex from the time of their very first awareness of their own sexuality. Chick, I won't take the time here to review this evidence since I know you are familiar with it. My own assessment is that it is very intriguing and provocative but far from certain. And even the evidence that appears to be supportive of genetic influence does not suggest that it is definitive, even for those homosexuals who appear to be that way from the time of earliest sexual awareness. For example, the twin studies which show a higher incidence of dual homosexuality among *identical* twins (who share the same genetics) than among *fraternal* twins (who do not) make clear that not all of the identical twin pairs studied demonstrated so-called dual homosexuality (a twin pair in which both twins are homosexual). Therefore, as has long been suspected, there are clearly influences other

than genetics involved in the eventual sexual orientation of a given person. But there is enough evidence for
the possibility of significant genetic influence to suggest
a caution about passing out "blame" for being homosexual.

All of this, I think, should discourage us from being
"judgmental" in our actions and behavior toward
homosexuals. When it comes to AIDS specifically, we
must be forthright about the kind of behavior that can
increase the risk for AIDS and equally forthright about
treating persons with AIDS as thoughtfully and compassionately as if they had any other serious disease.
Having said that, I recognize that society will be less
and less tolerant of any behavior (but especially sexual
or drug-related behavior) that leads to illnesses of any
kind that drain increasingly scarce medical funds and
resources. So what really worries me is not so much the
specific prejudice against homosexuality, though that
can indeed be serious, but the more general prejudice
that I see developing against those who are thought,
because of their sexual practices, to unfairly utilize
precious medical resources. And because drug abusers
in particular are also often members of minority
groups, the potential for social backlash is heightened. I
know this is something you worry very much about, so
I toss this back in your court for some further thoughts.
And I would like you to specifically comment on the

issue of AIDS testing for medical personnel, patients, and any other groups.

Sincerely,
Tim

———————————————

Dear Tim,

I knew that it wouldn't take you long to get around to asking about testing. When I was Surgeon General no issue provoked as heated debate as AIDS testing. At first look, it seemed so simple.

We had a killer disease on the loose, so why not just test everybody to see who has it? But that simplistic solution had many shortcomings. The main problem with mandating widespread testing was that we could offer no cure for AIDS. So, what would we do with the people who tested positive?

I'm sure you remember, Tim, that there were some people who wanted to take all who tested positive and either shoot them or herd them into concentration camps. But, our laws—and the Constitution—don't allow the government to round up people just because they are ill. Therefore, AIDS became an issue not only of health but also of civil rights. And AIDS became an issue that sometimes pitted our public-health concerns against our civil rights concerns. We have been torn between our desire to get a handle on the growth of this deadly disease and our commitment to our basic rights and liberties. Most public-health officials have always stressed the importance of *voluntary* testing for AIDS, but they have opposed mandatory testing. That's because in the absence of a cure for AIDS, widespread AIDS testing could result only in widespread discrimination against people who tested positive for the HIV virus even though it might be months or years before they displayed symptoms of AIDS. These people could lose job, home, insurance, and family. And these disasters could also injure that small number who would register a false positive on the test. Most Americans are not ready to shelve the Constitution—or basic decency—because of fear about AIDS.

Furthermore, mandatory AIDS testing would drive AIDS-infected people underground, away from the help and counseling that they desperately need. Specifically, AIDS-infected people need proper health care to manage the symptoms of their disease, and they need to be convinced to change their behavior so that they will not infect others. Health officials know that AIDS testing will serve its purpose only if it is voluntary and absolutely confidential.

But even though health professionals and society seem to have shelved the idea of widespread mandatory testing for AIDS, the issue of testing health-care workers and patients remains very much alive. I believe that routine testing of all patients is unnecessary and presents a greater burden to health-care institutions that outweighs the risk posed by the occasional AIDS patient. Although many people worry about the possibility of transmission of HIV in the hurried and often bloody conditions of hospital emergency rooms, the need for speedy attention in emergency rooms makes mandatory testing there nearly impossible. Emergency rooms, throughout the history of modern medicine, have always posed risks to those who serve there.

However, testing patients on an individual basis makes sense. If a hospital admits a patient who shows the marks and symptoms of an intravenous drug addict, and if the institution is in an area where AIDS has been reported, then it makes sense to test that patient for HIV. (Of course the hospital must follow whatever procedures the state laws require.) That kind of testing also makes sense for a homosexual patient with a history of sexual promiscuity and/or sexually transmitted disease as well as for a heterosexual patient with a history of multiple sex partners. Of course, such a policy means strong internal controls over test results and a restricted circle of personnel who have a "need to know" those test results. Hospital personnel should have the same zeal for protecting confidentiality as they have for HIV testing.

Those who oppose all patient testing will argue that doctors need to practice caution anyway, so why bother with testing? But in a high-risk area, if medical personnel are made tense about the possibility that they might be dealing with HIV-positive patients, the quality of the care they are providing can inadvertently be lowered.

Now, what about testing of health-care workers, about the possibility of transmitting the HIV virus not *from* the patient, but *to* the patient? Again, I think the current controls are adequate. This can be a highly emotional issue, but I am relieved that so far, reason has prevailed, and, for example, we have not allowed the isolated incident of AIDS transmission by a Florida dentist (a transmission that is still unexplained scientifically) to dictate public-health policy. However, if a physician or other health worker tests positive for HIV, I believe that person is obliged to report such information to his or her supervisor. From that point on, I suggest that a local committee of peers ought to decide what the infected person can and cannot do in health care. The American people must be assured that clear ethical standards are upheld, covering both the treatment of patients and the conduct of health workers. And, I might add, the longer that the health profession delays establishing ethical procedures concerning AIDS, the sooner the public will lose patience and turn to the courts. And the courts will, once again, have to step in and tell medicine what to do.

Tim, your last letter made clear your concerns about hostility toward homosexuals, especially from those critics who claim to base their views on the Bible. I believe that the Bible *does* condemn homosexuality as it does many other kinds of human behavior and that we should not be selective in the sins we excuse or ignore. And I don't agree with the implications of your remarks about a possible genetic element in homosexuality. Recently the press has been full of a new round of the "nature versus nurture" debate about homosexuality, but I'm not sure there is anything really new in all the discussion. The recent studies that reveal a somewhat higher incidence of dual homosexuality among identical twins seem to be more of an argument *against* the importance of genetics, or else the identical twins would *always* be the same in sexual orientation. Furthermore, the mere presence of a genetic element would not serve to *justify* homosexual behavior. It wouldn't surprise me if we eventually found genetic influences for all sorts of behavioral disorders. For example, the postulated genetic influence in alcoholism does not mean that alcoholism is no longer a disorder, nor does it keep alcoholics from being able to break that pattern of behavior. These issues, especially difficult enough to sort out when they touch both theology and biology, are made even more complicated by the political climate. For instance, the much-ballyhooed vote of the American Psychiatric Association to remove homosexuality from its list of emotional disorders had much more to do with political pressure than with new psychological insights.

But as you say, Tim, the "nature versus nurture" argument about homosexuality should not influence our view of AIDS patients. Our Judeo-Christian ethics and the best in the American humanitarian tradition commit us to care for them. AIDS patients, like leprosy patients of yesteryear, are abandoned by families, shunned by society, and are many times the victims of unwarranted abuse. Christians, even if convinced that homosexuality is a sin, should follow the example of Jesus, showing compassion to those who are ill.

Of course, our concern for protecting civil rights should not extend to protecting those people with AIDS who deliberately place others at risk. Many states have laws making it a felony to knowingly transmit a communicable disease, and these laws should be used to punish those whose deliberate, reprehensible behavior transmits their disease to others. But we can't rely on those laws to protect our citizens. It is up to each American to protect himself or herself against AIDS. That is why, in the absence of a cure or vaccine, we must stress education, education, and more education. And, the simple fact remains that most Americans will not get AIDS unless they decide to engage in personal behavior that places them at risk. I say "most" instead of "all" because we must remember that it is still possible for a monogamous man or woman to be unwittingly infected with HIV from a promiscuous or intravenous drug-using spouse. And, of course, there are those newborn babies infected with the HIV virus while being carried inside their mothers, or during delivery, and those infected by past blood transfusions.

I think that people who will not control their own high-risk behavior should realize that they face penalties. One penalty is the possibility of dying of AIDS. Another is the possibility that they will be tested for AIDS as a prior condition to receiving medical care.

AIDS could be the straw that breaks the back of America's chaotic health-care delivery system. It is already driving many inner-city hospitals toward bankruptcy, and its total cost will reach into the billions by the end of the decade. I am deeply concerned because no one seems to be planning to deal with the impact of AIDS on a health-care system already overburdened and under attack. So far AIDS has posed difficult ethical and economic questions for America, but the really difficult AIDS issues still lie ahead of us.

Of course, Tim, many of our ethical and economic concerns would be removed if a vaccine or a cure became available. Then, such highly emotional issues as testing and AIDS/sex education would be lessened. What do you see on the horizon as far as a vaccine or a cure for AIDS? And what do you see in the way of treatment?

Sincerely,
Chick

===============

Dear Chick,

Unfortunately, I must agree with your pessimistic outlook about future social problems related to the growing emotional and financial costs related to the care of AIDS patients. And I see no easy answers from medical science in the near future.

As you know, Chick, the HIV virus is a particularly diabolic virus because it is a member of a "family" of viruses—the so-called retro viruses—that infect host cells by entwining their genetic material with the genetic material of the host cell. That clever strategy of infectious attack makes it very difficult to eradicate the virus without destroying the host organism. Therefore, a "cure" in the sense of a once-and-for-all elimination of the virus in an infected person (as penicillin does to a bacterium) is currently impossible and very unlikely in the next several decades. *At best*, we might be able to achieve control of HIV infection in a given person with drug therapy that can prevent further infection in the body without serious side effects and at reasonable cost. (The model of some chronic diseases, like arthritis, might be appropriate: at least partial control of symptoms and the slowing of further progression but without actual cure.)

We have already made some progress toward that goal with the use of AZT and some newer drugs. Evidence suggests that the use of these drugs earlier in the infectious cycle can significantly delay the progression of the disease. But as you suggest, this therapy and the additional years of life obtained, add significantly to the cost of treating AIDS patients. That added cost comes not only from the direct treatment of the HIV virus infection but from the treatment of the many secondary diseases that can occur in a weakened AIDS patient. For example, one recent study indicates that for every one hundred hospital admissions for patients actually diagnosed with AIDS, there are an additional fifty-three admissions for problems in persons infected with the HIV virus who have not yet reached the stage of actual AIDS; in this study, by the way, the average *yearly* cost of AIDS patients was

$18,487 and the average yearly cost for HIV patients not yet progressed to AIDS was $11,010.

I am somewhat more optimistic about the possibility of an AIDS vaccine, though not much more. There are many technical problems in developing and testing such a vaccine, and the virus is changeable enough to foil vaccines based on current virus strains. But theoretically it should be easier to develop a vaccine that can prevent infection than to develop drugs that can eradicate the virus once it is in host cells. Even so, I personally do not believe we will see a practical preventive vaccine by the end of this decade. I would love to be wrong, but that's my best guess.

In short, I see very little hope that medical science via vaccine or drugs can make a major dent in the AIDS problem during the next decade. This means we must continue to emphasize prevention and plan for the onslaught of the costly care for AIDS patients that will explode in many of our major cities during the 1990s. I would predict the following social battles as we face that onslaught.

First, there will be tremendous pressure on drug companies to bring down the cost of drug therapy. The current drug costs are the result of a monopoly in which the free market does not operate—in which there is no competition to bring down the cost. I predict the government will have to step in to control such costs before they bankrupt the economy of certain cities and states. Second, there will be a growing emphasis on avoiding costly intensive care for AIDS patients as well as for many other clearly terminal patients. Good hospice care can provide more personalized human care at considerably less cost. Finally, there will be a growing backlash against persons who get sick because of lifestyle choices, and AIDS patients will be the prime example. I believe that religious leaders will have to lead the charge in preventing such a backlash and in providing the motivation—and maybe the funds—to care for such people.

In the meantime, we *must* emphasize the importance of prevention. The "good" news about AIDS, if there is any, is that we know how to prevent it, or more accurately, how to avoid getting it. AIDS does not strike in the shroud of mystery that surrounds many other diseases like breast cancer in women or prostate cancer in men. It almost always comes as the result of very specific activity, most of which is still a matter of personal choice (blood transfusions causing AIDS being obvious exceptions). In other words, AIDS does *not* "just happen" and it cannot just "happen to anybody." But it certainly can happen to anyone who engages in high-risk behavior and therein lies the real message: *High-risk behavior, not an unavoidable AIDS virus, is the enemy.*

Unfortunately, many in our society have concluded that high-risk behavior, at least high-risk sexual behavior, is a normal part of being human in the twentieth century. For them, we need to promote protected sex as long as they insist on continuing high-risk sexual activity. But we should not promote the cause of casual sex by false teaching that completely safe sex is possible through the use of protection such as condoms. The simple truth is that the only absolutely safe sex is sex with a partner that you are certain does not carry the HIV virus. You will notice that I did not include monogamous sex in that definition. Monogamous sex is obviously preferable to promiscuous sex in terms of lessening the risk of AIDS. But unless that one partner is certain to be free of HIV—that his or her sexual history is totally without possible exposure to AIDS— even monogamous sex is not totally safe. Given that so much potential sex in our society is not of this variety, what we must first talk about is abstinence. For those who insist on risky sexual encounters, we must encourage techniques that are best described as protected sex rather than "safe" sex.

In short, as you often say, AIDS is one problem to which traditional morality and modern science should speak the same message! We should use both avenues to get out the message about AIDS and always deliver it with compassion!

Sincerely,
Tim

*

Woe to those who make unjust laws,
to those who issue oppressive decrees,
to deprive the poor of their rights
and withhold justice
from the oppressed of my people.
ISAIAH 10:1, 2

4
Health Care

Dear Chick,

I know that both of us feel strongly that health care is a right, and that the lack of access to good health care for so many of our citizens is a moral outrage. I personally find it appalling that we and South Africa are the only industrialized countries in the world that do not guarantee at least basic health care for all our citizens. But American health care increasingly poses another moral question: How will we ration care even for those who now get basic care as we increasingly face a system that will no longer be able to afford everything for everyone at all ages? When I speak to the public about the need for health-care reform, I point out that if the current rate of inflation for health care were to continue unchanged, according to at least one calculation, in less than seventy years health care would consume one hundred percent of the gross national product! Obviously that can't happen, so the question is not *whether* we will do something about current costs, but only *what* we will do and *when* and *how* we will do it.

I waver in my own opinion about whether we should attempt a truly radical change in our health-care system or continue to tinker with the present system in hopes of effecting a collection of changes that will suffice. Before discussing that one, I will start us on a dialogue about various power centers in the present American health-care enterprise. (I avoid the word "system" because that implies far more coordination than actually exists.)

I begin with doctors, not only because we both are doctors, but because they have always been the most prominent symbols of health care in this country. More important, physicians control a significant portion of the dollars spent on health care—directly about nineteen percent through fees for professional services, indirectly up to another fifty percent through decisions to prescribe drugs, do surgery, order tests, and hospitalize. But as you well know, Chick, anyone who thinks that the total answer to the health-care crisis in this country is more control over doctors is dead wrong! In fact, even though doctors have been increasingly put under the heel of insurance company control in recent years, health-care costs have continued to rise dramatically in those very same years. That's because doctors are often simply responding to forces beyond their control such as the demands of consumers fueled by reports of new health technology in the media or the ordering of extra tests because of the fear of frivolous malpractice suits. However, in addition to those outside forces, doctors are also, unfortunately, too often responding to the normal human instinct to make more money by doing more of what they are trained and expected to do. Indeed, many critics say one of the most basic *financial* problems with our health-care system is the financial incentive to make doctors "doers" rather than "thinkers." Put another way, we are much more willing to pay doctors for doing a procedure than paying for the time to figure out what is really helpful and necessary—which may mean deciding *not* to do something.

Because of the present "fee-for-service" method of paying doctors, it is no accident that physicians are always trying to figure out how to do more "procedures" for which insurance will pay. This leads to the tremendous disparity of income between various specialists; physicians like internists, family physicians, and pediatricians who don't do as many procedures often make under $100,000 a year (before taxes) while surgical subspecialists (like ophthalmologists and urologists) and other physicians who do a lot of procedures can easily make over $500,000. It is also no accident that when attempts are made to control physician determined expenses in one area such as hospital stays, doctors quickly learn how to expand business in other areas such as out-patient procedures or ownership of lab and imaging facilities to which they refer their own patients.

Because of the inevitable tendency to do more procedures under the fee-for-service approach to physician compensation, I have come to believe that we must modify that system to reduce the temptation to simply do more to earn more. That will mean either a salaried system for physicians or a radical change in fees to reduce compensation for procedures that take less time and skill and which increase fees for important non-procedural care that allows the doctor to get paid for "thinking and talking time" with the patient. I know that the fee-for-service incentive can produce superb care and excellent physicians. However, I would also like to believe that if we provide the right financial and professional climate for physicians, such as the Mayo Clinic where physicians are on salary, there will be more than enough incentive to enter a profession that can still provide a wonderful opportunity for human service and intellectual stimulation. Along with much better than average salaries, that "climate" should include:

- removal of the threat of frivolous malpractice suits, thereby removing the huge financial and emotional costs of our present litigious approach.

- provision for medical education costs that will eliminate the massive debts now common among young doctors, debts that frighten away potential medical students from low income families and often drive doctors to choose high income specialties.

● radical change in the paperwork load that now often requires a doctor to spend more time on insurance forms than in taking care of patients.

Ultimately, it is in our own self-interest to make the medical profession so compelling that it will attract the best and brightest of our young people rather than encourage them to look to other pursuits that provide more reward with far less consumer hostility and far less training time. But in exchange for providing such a climate, society obviously has a right to hold physicians accountable for the quality of their work, and physicians must be subject to review and to the threat of demotion or dismissal just as anyone else in the workplace.

In short, I think we need a radical change in the financial ways in which we train and compensate physicians. I would love to hear your thoughts about how we might do this.

Sincerely,
Tim

Dear Tim,

I share your sense of indignation about the short-comings of the American health-care system. Sometimes I think that I should have issued another Surgeon General's Warning: "The American Health-Care System Could Be Hazardous To Your Health!" Although many Americans enjoy the finest health care in the world, too many of our fellow citizens see our health-care "non-system" (as you have rightly indicated) as a tyranny—more a curse than a blessing.

I've come to conclude that Americans have three incompatible demands for health care: We want immediate access to health care; we want the latest high-technology medicine; and we expect all this at a limited price. We can provide any two of these, but it may not be possible to get all three.

Since you have raised the role that physicians play in our health-care problems, I should say that I have some strong feelings on that issue—and a plan for change. There's no doubt that the current economic incentives for physicians under our "fee-for-service" system drive up costs and are not always in the patient's best interest. However, a heavy-handed plan to reduce economic incentive can have the effect of reducing not only medically *unnecessary* services, and I agree that there is too much done for the wrong reasons, but also reducing medically *necessary* services.

I don't think that doctors, as a group, are any better or any worse than other people, and I am still pleased by the highly dedicated physicians I meet in all kinds of medical practice as I travel around the country. But unfortunately, medicine offers great temptations that should be eliminated whenever possible. For example, the federal government should follow the lead of states that prohibit any physician from owning a facility to which a patient could be referred with financial profit going back to the referring physician.

As you know, Tim, just to keep in touch with the way they are thinking, I try to meet frequently with medical students as I travel. Not long ago in talking with a group of two hundred third- and fourth-year medical students at a West Coast university, the topic of salaried physicians came up. When I asked how many would be willing to go on a salary as medical doctors, only two students said they'd go on salary. I then sweetened the pot by promising them that they would never be falsely sued for a malpractice claim. Well, about half the group raised their hands on that one. Then, when I said that I would cancel their medical school debt in return for a salaried contract, all but two enthusiastically opted for salary. This points to a usually hidden factor in the health-care crisis: the crushing burden of medical school debt with which most doctors begin their practice.

Not only are we the only industrialized nation other than South Africa that doesn't provide access to good health care for all of our citizens, but we are also the only industrialized nation that doesn't subsidize the education of our physicians. Most medical students graduate from medical school with a debt (of anywhere from $40,000 to $150,000 or more) that shapes their practice of medicine for the next twenty years. You know what happens, Tim. That young man or young

woman who went to medical school with the high ideal
of serving people as the local doctor instead gets lured
into a lucrative medical specialty that allows him or her
to repay the debt and still raise a family. We have too
many physicians, and yet we go on producing too
many high-priced specialists in the suburbs, too few
primary-care physicians for rural or inner-city America.

We need a rational plan for the training and
allocation of physicians that addresses patient need,
not the staffing needs of hospitals or the financial needs
of medical school graduates overburdened with educational debt. I am deeply saddened by this process that
turns our most idealistic young medical students into
medical entrepreneurs with their eyes riveted to the
bottom line.

Now, Tim, I don't want to say that we are old
fogies, at least not a young lad like you, but I do think
that the doctor of today is not the doctor we need
tomorrow. The twentieth century doctor has served the
twentieth century very well, but I think we need a new
doctor for the twenty-first century. In fact, that was one
of the main reasons that I have signed on as a professor
at the Dartmouth Medical School. I'll be working in a
new institute designed to turn out a new kind of
medical student and a new kind of doctor.

Although we are only a few years from the twenty-
first century, we are still producing doctors according
to a model developed way back in 1910 with the Flexner
report on medical schools. Since then, medical schools,
in close association with research universities, have

stuck closely to the biomedical model for physician training. This has led to phenomenal progress in medical science and technology, which has benefited doctor and patient alike, but it may have shortchanged both society and the physician in the areas of ethics and human concern. I'd like doctors to be able to practice the *art* of medicine as well as the science of medicine. Although we'll always need and produce a number of research-oriented physicians, our need for the foreseeable future is for primary-care physicians, men and women more at home in outpatient clinics than in intensive care units.

We need to reach future doctors even *before* they enter medical school. Although most would-be doctors have already decided upon a medical career when they enter college, most premedical students know less about medicine than apprentice carpenters know about carpentry. We need to train our doctors through a mentoring system that puts them into contact with physicians and patients when they are still in college, so they can see if they are emotionally equipped, for example, to tell a thirty-year-old mother that her three-year-old daughter is not responding to the leukemia treatment and will die. We need to get medical students out into the community so that they can see firsthand the connection between illness and socio-economic conditions. We need to bring together pre-med students, med students, interns, and residents on a regular basis so that they can discuss and experience together not only the problems of medicine but also that euphoria and enthusiasm that medicine brings at its best. And we need to train a generation of physicians to practice prevention in their own lives and to teach prevention to their patients. My doctor of the future will reflect humanitarian values rather than greed. She or he will be inclined more toward low-tech medicine than high-tech. My doctor of the future will seek to know what works in medicine, and will strive to understand what patients want. And I trust she or he will be even more trusted and cherished than that family doctor your grandparents knew.

To produce the kind of doctors we need we must reform the malpractice mess that forces doctors and patients to view each other as potential legal adversaries. Malpractice reform requires legislation that is difficult to achieve because Congress and state legislatures include so many lawyers, and they are not likely to act against their own. Therefore it may take a grassroots rebellion to reform a medical malpractice system that spends more on legal and insurance overhead than on injury compensation, and then passes the bill along to all of us.

While physicians must be held appropriately accountable for actual malpractice, the constant threat of frivolous lawsuits drives up costs and makes medicine worse for everyone. How can doctors practice good medicine while wondering if they will next see their patients in court, flanked by their lawyers? Today's malpractice suits corrupt the basic emotional climate of medicine, making the doctor fear the patient that she or he wants to help.

As you know, Tim, the threat of a lawsuit always hanging overhead prompts physicians and hospitals to practice "defensive medicine," ordering medically unnecessary tests and procedures that increase the annual health-care spending by as much as fifteen billion dollars. But in spite of the spate of malpractice suits, our current system does not serve the patient very well. *The people who may be most deserving of compensation are not the ones who get it.* A Harvard study revealed that in New York the legal system was so intimidating that only one of twelve injured patients ever tried to sue. Meanwhile, other doctors are harassed wrongly.

We need some big changes in malpractice laws. First of all, the law should require compulsory arbitration before resorting to the courts. That would help patients and physicians alike. We also should disallow awards for alleged "pain and suffering" as well as contingency fees for attorneys, because they serve only to drive up the costs for everyone without serving the cause of justice. If we assigned a portion of malpractice insurance funds to provide no-fault coverage for adverse medical injury we could reduce further the need for costly court battles. As you know, Tim, most malpractice suits today are for *maloccurrence*, when a tragedy has occurred, even though the doctor has made the best effort.

Obviously, where there is malpractice—bad, or negligent practice—restitution and compensation are in order. But we doctors must do better in policing ourselves. Medicine must rid itself of those doctors who bring justified criticism to the profession. On the positive side, we need to teach young physicians to be better communicators, to understand informed consent, and to make their patients allies with them against the disease they fight together.

Malpractice reform is one area where we can achieve significant health-care change without getting into health care itself, without touching the patient. Another area is administration. Americans are angry when they realize how much of their health-care dollar—as much as twenty-five cents—goes to administration. As you said, it is common for a doctor's office to spend more time on the insurance form than the doctor spent with the patient. In this computer age it is insane to have more than eleven hundred different insurance forms clogging the system when we could use one electronic coding system.

But now I've opened what is perhaps the biggest can of worms: our chaotic and often shameful system of private and public-health insurance. What should we do to reform it? That should keep you busy for a while!

Sincerely,
Chick

───────────────

Dear Chick,

Before addressing our insurance mess as requested, I should tell you how much I like your basic ideas about medical education reform. We are clearly more in need of compassionate and wise primary-care physicians— the kind who can handle the vast majority of everyday medical problems—than we are in need of more high cost specialists. I wish you well in your endeavors at Dartmouth!

And your comments about the current litigious approach to medical injury are also on target. The simple truth is that the only ones truly benefiting from the present malpractice system are the trial lawyers (making big money on both sides of the battle by the way), those making their living off the court system or the malpractice insurance industry, and those relatively few patients who strike it rich in the courtroom. I remember one journalist who described our present malpractice system as the last great national lottery, and it is a lottery in which those with the most clever lawyers or the most emotional stories may hit it big while the majority of those injured by modern and often risky medical care get nothing. The obvious answer is a no-fault system based on rational decisions by experts, including not only doctors but lawyers, clergy, ethicists, and some common folk with common sense. And while most lawyers will fight such reform, sooner or later the emotional and financial cost of the present system will become so intolerable that society will demand a change.

Now to the insurance mess. The current hodge-podge of private and public-health insurance in this country surely constitutes one of the seven wonders of paperwork jungles in the history of the human race. Indeed, the current health-insurance paperwork routine would test the genius of Einstein and the patience of Job. But behind all this paperwork maneuvering lie two fundamental flaws in our philosophy of insurance: insurance tied to health status and employment.

With insurance cost tied to prior health status, those unlucky enough to get sick and therefore to most need health insurance are the ones who have the most difficulty obtaining it. Or they cause their company group rates to soar so dramatically that the very existence of small companies can be threatened. And with insurance tied to employment, losing a job can be catastrophic far beyond the loss of income. In countries where citizens give health care a more positive rating than in this country, insurance is not tied to health status or employment but is financed through general taxation, thus spreading the risk over as wide a base as possible. In contrast, the health insurance business in the United States is not a true insurance business but a "risk avoidance" business practiced by over one thousand different insurance programs, each trying to find the healthiest persons who will cost them the least. And it is this fragmented approach to insurance— multiple private plans with government trying to fill in the gaps with Medicare and Medicaid—that has led to a growing number of uninsured at the same time total health-care costs soar! And the administrative costs of this kind of system also continue to soar as these programs compete with each other for the "best" patients, each with their own marketing, accounting, and executive costs.

Clearly what is needed is some kind of national approach to health insurance. Now before you or anyone gets hot under the collar about "socialized medicine," let me make clear that I am talking about *universal health insurance, not a national health-care system*. There is a big difference! Britain, for example, has both and therefore represents what most people rightly label as "socialized medicine" (the government owning and operating health-care facilities). But almost all other industrialized nations, including Canada and Germany, provide a program of universal health insurance in which all citizens are guaranteed basic health care while the actual delivery of health care is left to nongovernment hospitals and doctors. In short, what I am advocating is some program in which national legislation guarantees basic health insurance to all citizens.

Now there are two basic ways of financing this, with a lot of variations in between. One would be a program in which basic care is guaranteed for all citizens through national legislation, but the actual care can be provided through any insurance program or health-care entity that wished to meet the standards of the federally mandated program; the financing of such care would continue through many and different private and public programs—a "multi-payer" system. The other basic approach is the "single-payer" plan in which a single entity, such as the national government via the tax system as in the case of Canada, collects and distributes the monies needed to provide medical care for all citizens.

I happen to favor the single-payer approach because of its potential for administrative simplicity. In Canada, for example, simple insurance forms are filled out by doctors, and the patient has no paperwork to worry about! No wonder Canada spends about one percent of its health-care dollars on paperwork costs versus about ten percent in this country. Just as important, doctors and patients are not wasting emotional energy trying to figure out how to play the insurance game and justify what they are doing for the patient. Now obviously there have to be controls on such a system to prevent unnecessary or excessive medical care. But that is one of the added potential benefits of a single-payer system, namely data collection under one system that allows monitoring for patterns of excess or abuse.

So why can't we do something similar in this country? The simple answer is that we have no political will or public demand strong enough to fight the groups with a vested interest in keeping the present insurance system. In fact, we do not have even enough political focus to implement answers that could help right now, such as federally mandated standards for coverage that would be similar for all insurance companies.

Obviously a move toward a simplified single-payer system would cost a lot of jobs in the health insurance industry, therefore, this change would have to be accomplished carefully and sensitively over a reasonable period of time to allow job retraining for those displaced. But wouldn't it make sense to have these people provide actual medical care instead of simply pushing paper aimed at denying care?

Your turn,
Tim

Dear Tim,

It didn't surprise me that you came out in favor of a single-payer health insurance system like the Canadian health-care system. There's little doubt that disenchantment with our system leads some people to see greener grass on the other side of the fence.

Some Americans wonder if we should have something like Great Britain's National Health Service, where all health care is run by the government. Others seem intrigued with the German system, more like ours, but with *non-profit* insurance companies and national limits on annual health-care expenditure. But for many people the most attractive foreign example is also the closest: the Canadian system, where health insurance is controlled by the provincial governments, subject to national guidelines and limits. My hunch is that the growing infatuation with foreign national health plans is based more upon dissatisfaction with

our system than upon any real understanding of
another one.

It is true that Canadians are much happier with
their health-care system than we are with ours. They
have reason to be proud that all their people have
access to care and that its cost is covered by government insurance. And as you say, Tim, Canada's health-
care administrative costs are only a fraction of ours.
Canada is proud that it manages to provide basic health
care to all its citizens. I'm ashamed that we don't.

But it is also true that the Canadian level of
satisfaction seems to be leveling off and even declining.
The Canadian system worked rather well at first, but
now it faces a new decade of costly problems that were
not present when the system started: the need to
replace aging medical equipment and technology, the
impact of AIDS, and (like the USA) a growing elderly
population.

Many Americans don't realize that any national
health plan is based upon *planned scarcity*. Although
most Canadians have no trouble getting routine medical care, they tolerate what Americans would regard as
unbearable waiting lines for things like bypass surgery,
MRI scans, and hip replacements. National systems of
health care eventually become bureaucratic, unrespon-
sive to patients, and finally they bring rationing and
waiting in lines. Americans do not queue up patiently
for anything, especially for medical care. The world-
wide experience over the last generation seems to show
pretty clearly that when government economic controls

are applied to health, they prove—in time—to be detrimental. The controls are based on planned scarcity and lead to an erosion of quality, innovation, and creativity.

Research is often the first to be hurt. Americans desire not only affordable health care but also medical advances. But medical research is not cheap, and someone must pay for it. Americans are not likely to tolerate health-care savings if it means skimping on Alzheimer's research. Canada has enjoyed the luxury of often relying upon the United States for medical technology and medical research.

And many critics of the Canadian health-care system maintain that it could not continue to function even at its current rationed efficiency if the United States and our health-care facilities were not just south of the border. I know, Tim, that it is hard to pin down all the stories about how many Canadians seek surgery in Buffalo, Seattle, or Boston. And I know that some people counter by claiming that U.S. citizens migrate north to get the long-term care they can't afford here. But there is no dispute that Canadian health-care costs are beginning to soar at a rate as fast as ours.

Although we have much to learn from Canada, I don't think that we can solve our problems by buying an import. Each national culture is different, and health-care systems grow within a culture. That's why you get different systems in Canada, Germany, Great Britain, and the United States. Canadian society and American society are more similar than many, but there are also profound differences in social expectations and political realities.

I think it ironic that at a time when socialist regimes are collapsing all around the world and American disenchantment with politics and government seems at an all-time high, so many Americans clamor for the government to take over the health-care mess. I think this reflects the degree of our frustration rather than our confidence in the federal government. I could joke with you and ask if you would favor a federal health-care system run like the postal service. But you'd probably ask me how I'd like it if the mail were delivered by the fragmented and inefficient health insurance industry. Right?

Sincerely,
Chick

Dear Chick,

You're right, that's exactly what I would say. Actually, I think our postal system gets a bad knock when compared to our health-care system. Many citizens in this country have a far better chance of getting a letter on time than getting needed medical care in early and low-cost fashion when it might prevent the need for more complicated and costly care later on. For example, we Americans think nothing of cutting back on infant immunization programs and then paying hundreds of thousands of dollars for the intensive care bill that results when a child gets deathly ill as a result of not being immunized! In fact, that's a big part of our problem: we literally "think nothing" about so much of what we are doing—or not doing— in health care that we have a monster on our hands consuming huge amounts of money without any real plan or understanding about what makes the most sense in spending that money. And at least Canada has made a thoughtful attempt to provide the most impor- tant basic care to all its citizens before worrying about high-tech medicine that will benefit only a few. I think it takes a lot of chutzpah for American political and medical leaders to criticize a health plan that does that! So I am happy to see you acknowledge that Canadians have a right to be proud of what they have accom- plished.

I became a believer in the fundamental premise of the Canadian system after doing a TV report comparing health care in the U.S. and Canada. To make the comparison come alive in human terms, we asked the family practice organization in the state of New York and the comparable organization in Ontario to pick a "typical" family practice in each location. We asked each practice to pick a "typical" family in their practice, and we spent a day in each location interviewing the physicians and families that had been picked. The two physicians in New York described a typical primary- care practice struggling to meet the demands of pa- tients and paperwork. The doctors in New York had actually calculated that their office spent more time in billing and related administrative activities than in patient care. The family picked in New York was a young family (two parents, two young children) that fell through the typical cracks of insurance coverage in this country: too rich to qualify for Medicaid but too poor to buy health insurance. So when their youngest child was about to be delivered, the husband had to argue with the business office of the local hospital about how they were going to pay their bills while his wife-in-labor waited anxiously in the lobby.

By contrast, the physicians in Ontario hired a clerk to come in one night a week to do all their billing paperwork: one simple form for all patients. Even though the physicians' gross income was considerably less than their counterparts in New York, their net income was almost the same because their overhead was so much lower. By coincidence, the family in Canada turned out to be a mirror image of the family in the States—same aged parents with two kids the same ages. But when *their* youngest child had been delivered, they walked into the hospital, showed their government insurance card and, in the words of the father, "They whisked us upstairs."

Now I agree that Canada is having the same problem of escalating costs that is plaguing all industrialized countries with growing high-tech medicine combined with population growth, especially among the elderly. Without some controls, that's a formula for financial disaster. But at least Canada has in place a system that can get a handle on those costs and try to deal with the problem in a rational fashion rather than in the irrational way we simply drum thirty to forty million Americans out of our health insurance "system." In other words, I'd rather have the *planned* scarcity that you accurately describe as the Canadian approach than the *unplanned* scarcity we have in this country that denies so many of our citizens the care they should have. And you are right to question all the stories about Canadians dying because they can't get needed care; when you ask Canadian health-care experts about that, they laugh at the hysteria of the American press and the American Medical Association in reporting so many unsubstantiated rumors. And I admire—rather than criticize—Canadians for being more patient and less selfish than we are when it comes to demanding everything right away and right on our own street corner. We Americans can learn from our Canadian neighbors about capping our greedy appetite for immediate access to the latest medical technology.

I do worry that medical research becomes a tempting target in any cost control effort. Some research—that which is designed to turn out new gadgets or drugs simply to make new profits for drug and technology companies—needs to be curbed. But we *must* support that kind of research that helps us decide what really works in cost effective fashion in health care and research that provides true advances.

And finally in response to your comments about socialist systems, as I said earlier, there is a big difference between countries like Britain and Sweden (in which the government actually "owns" the health-care system) and most other industrialized countries in which the government guarantees health care for all citizens but leaves the actual delivery of health care to the private sector. It is the latter approach I favor, and it is not "socialist."

Speaking of government insurance inevitably raises the controversial Medicare and Medicaid programs. I assume that you have some thoughts about these government programs.

Sincerely,
Tim

Dear Tim,

I do indeed. But before I get into government insurance plans, let me go back to Canada and say that one of the reasons that Canadians are satisfied with their system is that fifty percent of their doctors are primary-care physicians—versus only twenty percent in the United States. We must change that!

Often I think the federal track record in the health-care business is dismal. With Medicare and Medicaid, the government made health-care promises to the elderly and to the poor, but has not kept those promises. Medicare, the government health insurance for the elderly, is one of the most decent things that this country has done to remove much of the fear and uncertainty from elderly life. But Medicare is full of holes. While I think that it is appropriate for wealthy older Americans to dip into their own ample assets before Medicare kicks in, other senior Americans find Medicare inadequate. Medicare often does not cover the drugs that elderly citizens need to safeguard their health, and it makes no provision for the long-term care that many of us will need someday. While I encourage families to do more than they are now doing to care for grandparents, nonetheless there are times when institutional care is warranted and too many Americans see it consume their life savings and their home. Medicare needs to be reformed so that it becomes economically equitable, economically viable, and medically appropriate.

Tampering with Medicare makes many ripples; in 1990 Medicare spending amounted to 110 billion dollars. That also amounts to forty percent of all hospital income, and accounts for twenty-five percent of the average doctor's income. Medicare needs not only financial reform but also conceptual reform that includes education about appropriate care in the context of decision making at the end of life. And, unlike you, I can say from personal experience that it wouldn't hurt to make those frustrating Medicare forms a little more user-friendly.

As for Medicaid, I think we should replace it entirely. Medicaid, the federal insurance program designed for the poor, excludes most of the poor by calling them too rich. (In Alabama, for instance, a family of three with an income of $1,460 a year can be

too rich to qualify for Medicaid.) Medicaid pays physicians inadequately, so more and more doctors simply
refuse to see Medicaid patients. The health insurance
program originally designed for the nation's poor now
covers only one half of them. Medicaid should be
replaced by a basic primary care and catastrophic care
health insurance program affordable to all Americans.
Although I do not favor *universal* government insurance, I think that there is a role for government in
providing tax-supported insurance for those in real
need. As Abe Lincoln once said, whatever people need
and can afford, they should pay for, but the government has to cover the rest.

I think that sums up my approach to the health
insurance nightmare: some combination of private and
government insurance, rather than a Canadian type
system that could stifle the creativity and variety that
has the potential to make American health care the best
in the world.

Right now, as you have made so clear, Tim, our
private health insurance structure often operates like a
shell game, a national disgrace. But I think it can be
reformed rather than abolished. I'm no defender of the
insurance industry, but we probably need to face the
reality of its political clout. Americans may rail against
the insurance companies—and the companies often
deserve these attacks—but when laid-off insurance
workers turn out to be family members and neighbors,
then I'm afraid the tune will change.

I think that we can turn the variety in the insurance

business to the advantage of the consumer/patient. To do this, we'll need comprehensive insurance reform on state and federal levels. Here's what I'd like to see happen:

- Provision of an alternative to employer-provided insurance that has a bigger pool so that we no longer burden workers and our economy by "job lock" that keeps people in jobs they wish to leave but can't, just because they are afraid to lose their health insurance.

- We should level the playing field by replacing our currently regressive employer tax exemptions for insurance with tax credits or vouchers that link individual insurance premiums to ability to pay. (This could replace Medicaid.) Pre-existing health conditions should not exclude people from insurance coverage.

- State legislatures should eliminate state-mandated insurance benefits, which are usually based on politics, not on health requirements. For example, there is no reason that every insurance plan in a state must cover the same wide range of alternative procedures. People should be able to pick a plan that best suits their individual and family circumstances.

- A flexible system of private insurance including higher deductibles and tax-free medical savings plans would discourage unnecessary procedures and overutilization, because people think twice before they spend their own money.

• It seems sensible to me to link the price of insurance premiums and even insurance coverage itself to behavior. Why should the rest of us subsidize the insurance of people who knowingly and continually place themselves at greater risk for illness and accident by smoking, driving after drinking, not wearing seat belts, and so on? And of course I think that we should have even *higher* tobacco and alcohol taxes to pay for health-care costs attributed to those deadly substances.

• Above all, the basic principle of health insurance needs to be changed. Instead of serving as a pass-along-payment-mechanism, health insurance should offer protection against catastrophic illness and incentive for timely primary care and prevention. Instead of competing with each other about whom they will exclude from coverage, insurance companies should compete on how well they bring sick and healthy people together in pools to make affordable health insurance available to every American.

Through a combination of insurance plans, we need to make sure that no citizen is without basic health-care insurance. The health problems of the uninsured, if ignored by society now, will be borne by society later because there is a clear connection between having no medical insurance and then developing serious health problems. A study published in 1991 showed that those hospital patients with no health insurance are three times more likely to die in the hospital than patients with private health insurance. The thirty-five million Americans without health insurance do not get as much health care as they should, and when they do get it, the costs are passed along to others.

Of course, the reason that thirty-five million Americans have no health insurance is that it costs too much, and insurance costs too much because health-care costs too much. I realize, Tim, that simply providing everyone with insurance won't solve the problem, because universal insurance by itself provides no incentive to control costs. In fact, complete insurance coverage tends to make costs escalate rapidly because people think that "someone else is paying." I know most cost-control measures simply aimed at cost-containment have failed. It's like squeezing a balloon: Compression at one place just leads to expansion somewhere else. But maybe you have some workable plans for cost control.

Sincerely,
Chick

Dear Chick,

I wish your hopes for reform of the private insurance industry could come to fruition. But I am far less optimistic than you. I agree that politically it may be the only way to go for the moment. But I predict that as costs keep rising, something more radical will have to be done than simply tinkering with the present hodge-podge of private and government mix. (Even the editor of the *Journal of the American Medical Association* admits we are headed for a "meltdown" in health-care costs if we don't do something soon.) In short, I think we will need some kind of national health insurance program that develops a comprehensive plan of basic health care for all Americans, combined with a plan for cost controls and rationing. Now, finally, I have mentioned those two politically explosive concepts, so I had better explain what I mean and why I think that any attempt at health-care reform is ultimately doomed without these two features.

First, the need for cost controls. As I explained earlier, *there is currently no truly effective incentive to control costs, and the usual forces that control costs in a free market system do not exist when it comes to the health-care marketplace.* Put simply, when it comes to health care, there is a constantly growing demand with a constantly growing supply of health-care providers and attendant products to match the demand. The usual market force provided by fully informed consumers able to say "no" is not possible: When people are sick or are worried about becoming sick, they simply want what they think is the best and the latest care available, especially when someone else is paying for it. The solution is to limit demand in morally appropriate ways and to assume more direct responsibility for health-care costs rather than assume that someone else will simply pay the bill.

As a first step we must develop a national budget process for health care just as we have for education, defense, and so on. In other words, we must put a cap on how much we can afford to spend for health care. I am *not* saying that we currently spend too much. That may shock you, given all my concern about rising costs. I am certain, as you are, that we waste a significant amount of our current expenditure on health care and that we spend too much of it foolishly. But assuming that we can get a handle on that problem, we may as a society decide to spend even more than we do now. In fact I think when a true budget process is applied to health care as part of an overall discussion about the national budget, Americans may well vote to spend an even larger share of the national budget on health and correspondingly less on other areas such as defense. But the key is to engage in a rational national debate about how much we want to spend rather than the current "spend as we go" approach without any controls.

The German health-care system may serve as a model in this regard. First, via a very public process well covered by the media, Germans undergo what amounts to a budget process to decide how much they can spend on health care each year. The basic philosophy has been to tie any growth in the budget for health care to a comparable growth in income and wages. Put simply, in recent times Germans have not allowed the inflation rate for health care to outstrip the general inflation rate. Second, once these overall budget guidelines are established, associations representing physicians and hospitals and other health-care providers negotiate with associations representing insurance funds to work out actual fee schedules for services and hospitalizations costs. While physicians are often unhappy with the results, they do acknowledge that they are real partners in the process and that they still have great clinical freedom to do what they think necessary without having to constantly justify their choices via insurance paperwork and phone calls (as do American physicians).

However, simply putting a cap on expenditures is not enough. Whatever money we spend should be spent wisely, which means rationing or prioritizing— deciding how we should spend the money. As you well know, Chick, the state of Oregon has proposed such a plan for part of its Medicaid population, suggesting that it makes more sense to give as much basic care to as many poor people as possible rather than simply to pay for everything American technology has developed for a fewer number of people. In fact, according to the Oregon proposal, over 100,000 poor people in the state who now get no Medicaid coverage would get a rather comprehensive package of basic care.

The heart of the controversial Oregon Medicaid proposal is a list of 709 diagnostic and treatment techniques that are ranked in the order of their medical effectiveness and importance. This ranking was accomplished by a state panel composed of both doctors and nonphysicians who did their ranking after a series of community meetings held over an eighteen-month period designed to get input from the public. Once having ranked the diagnostic tests and treatments, the Oregon legislature could decide how far down the list a given amount of money would go into providing care for all who qualify according to their poverty guidelines.

The Oregon plan, of course, has been subject to intense scrutiny and criticism because it seems to represent "rationing for the poor" as though we don't have such rationing now! And in one sense it does represent rationing; it is an attempt to decide how best to use ultimately limited resources. And like many, I am uneasy about an attempt to impose only on the poor a process that I believe we must institute for all our citizens. But the charge of "rationing for the poor" is also misleading because it does not acknowledge that this process provides at least some basic care to many poor people who now get nothing.

There is much more to the very comprehensive and thoughtful overall health-care reform that Oregon is trying to institute, but I believe the element of prioritizing health care is so basic to any reform that it should be a part of any national reform. I have spent considerable time looking at the ranking of the 709 diagnosis-treatment categories in the Oregon Medicaid plan, and I would say simply that it makes a great deal of sense to anyone who knows what is cost effective in our current range of treatment choices.

Obviously, any individual physician would quarrel with some of their ranking choices, but overall they have done an excellent job of putting important and helpful items toward the top and less helpful ones toward the bottom. For example, prenatal care is toward the top as an obviously beneficial expenditure both for the pregnant woman and society, but fertility treatment is toward the bottom as something less vital to society's needs. Another example: Vigorous early treatment for AIDS is toward the top but expensive intensive care unit treatment for end-stage AIDS is not.

Now, these two processes—budgeting and setting priorities—taken together are going to confront us eventually with some very hard choices. I think that we can buy a considerable amount of time with some of the reforms we have discussed so far: eliminating fraud and waste, cutting down on administrative costs, eliminating the costs of defensive medicine, and so forth. But sooner or later we will come up against the limits of what we can afford as a society, and then the hard choices will begin. For example, at what point—if ever—do we decide we cannot afford to keep a very premature newborn on expensive intensive care machines that may produce a severely impaired child? Or what, if anything, should we do about the fact that one out of every seven dollars now spent for health care is spent for care in the last six months of life? And what about the tough choices in between these life extremes? I am not suggesting we have to come up with answers for these problems right now, but we had better start thinking about morally acceptable ways at least to discuss them.

In short, I think any reform plan that does not include budgeting and setting priorities—that's a less emotional word than "rationing"—is doomed to failure. Continuing to tinker with the present system is like putting a band-aid on a gaping wound. We need some bold new ways of coping with our present crisis. Your turn.

Sincerely,
Tim

P.S. I agree with your idea of asking people to pay more for their bad habits—both through increased insurance costs and direct taxes on the products. And I would be willing to consider extending that idea to pregnant women who engage in bad health practices during pregnancy!

====================

Dear Tim,

Until very recently, health-care "rationing" was something no one even wanted to talk about, much less implement. But, as you say, the Oregon proposal to ration Medicaid services has opened a very heated debate. I think that we should be honest and admit that we are already rationing medical care at almost every level without ever discussing it or devising a policy. All you have to do is observe how a patient enters the health-care system through an overburdened urban

emergency room, and you'll find limited choices—
rationing—every step of the way.

Although I am in agreement with the goals of the
sponsors of the Oregon rationing program—accessible
health care for all citizens—I think that their rationing
plan is not the way to achieve these goals. Well over a
century ago, many Americans rushed to the conclusion
that they could solve all their problems simply by
following the Oregon Trail. For most, it didn't work out
that way, bringing even more sorrow and suffering as
they fell by the wayside or had their hopes dashed. I do
not think that a twentieth or twenty-first century
Oregon Trail will lead us to where we wish to go.

However, there is much in the Oregon plan that
demands our attention. The plan's main sponsor,
Oregon senate president John Kitzhaber, himself an
emergency room physician, is right on target when he
says that Medicaid not only excludes too many poor
people, but also it *excludes* too many right treatments
and *includes* too many wrong ones. The Oregon plan
properly realizes the fiscal impossibility of providing
every citizen immediate access to every available medical service at no direct personal cost, and this may be its
greatest contribution to the health-care debate.

But, I don't think that the Oregon plan *can* work.
And I don't think the Oregon plan *should* work. The
American health-care system may not function correctly now, but Oregon will not make things right. Two
wrongs do not make a right. Replacing our unfair *de
facto* rationing scheme with an unfair *planned* rationing

scheme is not progress. The rationing plan affects only those Oregonians poor enough to receive Medicaid. Also, while some Medicaid patients would have to give up some services to get others, the rationing plan will not apply to elderly, disabled, blind, and long-term care Medicaid patients. They will continue to receive full benefits, and they already consume three-fourths of Medicaid funds.

The patients most affected by the rationing plan will be welfare mothers and children. Henry Waxman, chairman of the U.S. House of Representatives Sub-committee on Health and the Environment, says, "It is hard to accept that the first people to have their health care rationed is a politically powerless group that has the least health care to begin with. This is one instance in which it is wrong to send women and children first."

It seems to me that the Oregon plan uses the most vulnerable people of society in a social experiment that no one else is required to enter. Furthermore, treat-ments for individual patients should not be based on "society values" but on "patient values," which often differ from "society values" and even from physician values.

I am concerned about what a rationing plan will do to our national ethics and to the doctor-patient relation-ship. Our American values of fairness and equality commit us to providing basic care to everyone as the Oregon plan proposes, but our compassion for the individual in need can undo that consensus. You remember, Tim, when the initial interest in the Oregon rationing plan turned to hostility when television viewers saw little seven-year-old Colby Howard begging for money for a life-saving transplant no longer available to him under Oregon Medicaid? Colby didn't raise the money, he didn't get the operation, and he died. Rationing may seem rational only as long as it remains abstract. Americans are less moved by statistics about the need for prenatal care than by families begging with tin cups at the supermarket so that their child can get an operation.

Above all, I think we can accomplish the goals of the Oregon plan without the bitter pill of rationing if instead we focus on *resource reallocation* and *outcomes research*. Like most places, Oregon demonstrates a wide variation in the availability and use of medical facilities. Some communities, for instance, use many more hospital beds (and all the attendant services and personnel) than other cities use. But the people in those cities do not seem to live longer or healthier lives than the people who live in cities with fewer hospital beds. Reallocating this excess capacity and investment would more than pay for the services unavailable under the ration plan.

Now, Tim, I realize that rationing might make easier politics than reallocation because it is easier to ration the health care of the poor than to reallocate the health care of the middle class and the affluent. Reallocation is not easy. Each excess hospital bed to be moved takes about ten or twelve jobs with it. But, if we are looking for long-term solutions, if we are faced with the choice between rationing of care and reallocation of resources, we have the ethical imperative to try first the reallocation. It defies common sense and it violates our ethical integrity to focus so much of our attention on rationing health care for *some* people in *some* places when we have excess capacity health care for *other* people in *other* places.

But we need more than reallocation. As you know, Tim, for all our "scientific medicine," we are too much in the dark about what really works in medicine and what doesn't. The choice of medical treatments is made in a shockingly capricious manner, reflecting not the conclusions of science but the hunches and practice patterns of local physicians. For example, in one little Vermont town, seventy percent of the kids got their tonsils removed, while not far down the road in a similar Vermont town the tonsillectomy rate barely reached seven percent. Somebody's out of line. We need to provide doctors with much clearer evidence about what works, what doesn't work, and what remains uncertain. And then doctors must share that information with their patients so that the patients can make truly informed decisions that they will have to live with.

We need to make funds available for a systematic program of this kind of outcomes research to enable patients and physicians to know the outcomes of all medical treatments. If we were to allocate one-fourth of a cent of each insurance dollar to fund outcomes research and if we were to make sure the values of the patient played a central role in the choice of medical treatment, we would achieve lower costs and higher quality health care for everyone. In my opinion, thirty percent of current diagnostic and treatment procedures is medically unnecessary. If we cut that fat alone, we would save more than 200 billion dollars, which would more than pay for what the uninsured lack. Outcomes research is the wave on which health policy reform rides at the moment.

So, we agree that we need reform and a lot of it. We don't agree—and maybe we haven't even made up our own minds about exactly what we must do first. I do not favor totally scrapping the system we have now. Because of its diversity, it is potentially the best in the world. But we have a crisis on the way, and unless we reform before the system reaches chaos or collapse, we will get either government medicine, exorbitantly expensive and insensitive to patient needs, or we will have private medicine run amok.

There is, of course, a reason that change comes so slowly. There are many interest groups associated with health care who are more concerned about their own *wealth* than about the American people's *health*. Many of the entrenched people who pocket a large share of the more than 800 billion dollars spent annually on health care fight any change that might threaten them. And their political donations seem to buy them protection. The millions of Americans who have the most to gain from health-care reform—the poor and the sick— are unorganized and unfunded. The interest groups who have the most to lose from health-care reform are well-organized and well-funded.

Although real reform cannot succeed without national leadership and federal participation, health-care reform, like most significant social reform in American history, can start with the individual states, where a variety of solutions can be tried out.

The states can move forward even while the federal government fiddles. In each facet of the health-care complex we need imaginative, sensitive, effective reform to meet a variety of problems, and I think that in the immediate future we will see incremental reforms on the state level. This *may* be the way out of our current mess, although the risk of incremental reform is that without an overall vision of where we should go, each incremental reform could take us in the wrong direction. Panicky and poorly conceived legislation could place on our backs a burdensome system that could take a generation to relieve.

And reform will take time. If all people concerned with health-care reform were of good will (which they are not), if the principal health-care players could agree on a single plan (which they cannot), if everything went smoothly (which it never does), it would still take a decade to get from where we are to where we want to be, even if we'd improve year by year along the way. Tim, do you think that reform can come more easily or more quickly?

Sincerely,
Chick

Dear Chick,

That's a tough question you ask. There is a fine line between pessimism and realism. You are certainly realistic about our current health-care problems and the self-serving resistance to solving them. But I think you are too pessimistic about the willingness of Americans to change *if* they are told the truth about what is wrong and what needs to be done, and *if* the proposed solutions are fair to everyone.

Now that requires the kind of political leadership that we just haven't seen so far, at least when it comes to health-care reform. And I would like to believe that if the president of this country were willing to lay out the problems and propose bold and fair solutions, the American people would respond positively.

I also believe that many Americans would respond to a call by churches, synagogues, and other volunteer groups to provide health care. After all, before the days of government programs, these groups were the major providers of charity in general, including health care for the poor.

There are basically two ways to deal with the American health-care crisis. One is to keep hoping that it will go away, and to deal with it piecemeal only as glaring wounds become impossible to ignore. The other way is to propose a series of basic changes that would call upon all the elements of our health-care enterprise—doctors, lawyers, insurance companies, drug and product companies, hospitals, and all of us as consumers—to make the kind of sacrifices that will serve the common good and therefore provide at least basic health care to all our citizens at a cost we can afford. I must reluctantly agree with you that political considerations will probably prevent doing the latter, but I keep hoping that some political leader will come along with the courage to do it right. I might also add that biblical teaching about equality, fairness, and special care for the poor ought to mobilize the church.

Here is what I think it would take to do it right. The Congress and the president should appoint a National Board of Health Care, composed of the best brains and hearts available and give them broad powers to develop national policy guidelines to be implemented by the states through local health-care groups such as HMOs, hospital plans, insurance companies—i.e., any group that would meet the federal guidelines. Included in the mandate of the National Board should be the power to:

- propose a national budget for health care and a basic package of insurance coverage that must be provided to all citizens. (Rich people can always buy more with private funds; I don't like the idea but I see no way to avoid it and I can live with it as long as everyone is guaranteed basic services.)

- supervise a process of annual negotiation with doctors, hospitals, drug companies, and so forth, for the rates and fees to provide those services and allocate the money for health care collected through the general tax system to the fifty states according to their size and the medical needs of their particular populations.

- determine the needs for medical personnel and equipment in these states thereby putting an overall cap on the numbers and kinds of doctors and other health-care personnel that we produce year-by-year.

- set guidelines for the insurance package that must be provided by any and all health-care providers in the states and mandate a uniform and simplified billing system that will slash current administrative costs.

- oversee a process of outcomes research that will allow setting priorities for medical procedures according to cost and medical effectiveness, the results of which can be used in determining the amount and kind of medical care the American people feel they can afford.

With these guidelines and processes in place, any group of health-care professionals that is willing to meet these guidelines can compete for patients on a "providing the best service" basis. The payment structure developed according to national guidelines must allow varying payments per person on an annual basis according to that person's age and medical condition, *which means that no health plan should be allowed to turn down anyone who applies for care through their plan.* Such a system will allow competition for the provision of the best service but *not* for finding the largest number of "low risk" patients while ignoring sicker and therefore more costly patients.

In short, I am proposing a program of universal health insurance according to federal guidelines to be administered by the states and delivered by local health-care groups. In very brief and simplistic form, that's my "plan." I realize that it is far more radical than yours, but I also recognize that our goals are very much the same. And ultimately it may be "matters of the heart" rather than the specific plan details that count the most when it comes to health-care reform. So I'll give you the final word on this subject since you have lived through more of the human experience with health care than I have.

Sincerely,
Tim

Dear Tim,

I'm pleased to see that your plan for health-care reform has as its objectives many of the same ones I have already mentioned. And while I like much of what you propose, I simply don't think that your plan for universal health insurance will work, at least not in the foreseeable future. Although I think you're right when you say that all the groups involved in the health-care enterprise will need to make short-term sacrifices for long-term gain, I don't see anyone on the horizon who has the ability to lead them—or embarrass them—into doing what they need to do.

I like your idea of the president and the Congress's appointing a National Board of Health Care. But I don't think it's going to happen, because I tried hard—and failed—to make it happen. In a private conversation with George Bush I urged him to appoint the kind of board or commission you recommend, and I have repeated the idea from lecterns all across the country as well as in an essay I wrote for *Newsweek*. So far, nothing has happened. And Congress, currently held hostage to the entrenched interest groups defending the status quo, is not likely to vote for a national board that has sweeping powers.

Let's face it, Tim. It's very difficult to get sweeping reform in this country, and part of the reason is that the founding fathers wrote a constitution that makes it difficult for the federal government to force universal change on the states. Even in national programs like federal welfare assistance and Medicaid, the states have fought for the right to do it their way. I see any universal health plan getting splintered by the fifty states. And I'm afraid that it might bring out, not the best but the worst in the American character, especially if suburban and rural Americans resist the idea of their tax dollars going to meet the daunting health needs of inner city America.

I think your idea about a national budget for health care as we have for education and defense might eventually take hold. But your comparisons illustrate the inherent problems. In health care, as in education, Americans tend to think that local folks know best what local schools and local hospitals should provide, not distant bureaucrats inside the Washington beltway. And your comparison to the defense budget does not reassure those of us concerned about cost escalation and even outright fraud.

I think it would be a costly mistake, Tim, to launch any kind of universal government health insurance program until we find more effective ways to ferret out the fraud and abuse that already plague our current Medicare and Medicaid programs. As you know, some investigators claim that the pervasive fraud in Medicare makes the Savings and Loan scandal look like child's play.

I know, Tim, that you think I'm too pessimistic about government health-care insurance plans and that you think I'm too optimistic about our ability to force the necessary reforms and justice upon private insurance plans so that they can meet the needs of citizens currently excluded. But I think that the variety and resourcefulness within our current health-care enterprise and insurance system, if made ethically accountable, hold more promise than an enlarged government system. (I can't help noticing, Tim, that when we want to get one of these letters to each other in a hurry, we send them not by the government postal service but by a private express carrier!)

And finally, Tim, as enormous as the problems with our health-care complex might seem, we may be too *narrow* in our focus. We need to understand the problems and find the solutions, not just in the health-care system, but in society itself. American health problems stem from diseases not only of the body but also of society, especially the disease of poverty. I know that you agree that poverty lies at the root of most of our public-health problems: drug abuse, AIDS, alcohol abuse, malnutrition, smoking, communicable diseases. Most of the discouraging statistics about our nation's health, such as our high infant mortality rate, come from the impoverished millions who exist on the fringes of our affluent society. We must remember in our efforts to provide health care for all Americans that health care is not the same thing as health, and that health-care expenditures that take away from our efforts to reduce overall poverty may not result in greater health.

The shameful prevalence of poverty in our rich country is, unfortunately, a reflection not only of our economics but also of our ethics. I'm sure that you share my dismay at the erosion of an ethical consensus about many issues in American society. Perhaps we should have started our discussion here, because I don't see how we can enact the sweeping reform we need in health care until we first agree on the basic values and ethics upon which our health-care system— and our society—is based, and from which our society derives its moral power. If we could reach an ethical consensus, many of the economic and political problems of health-care reform would be easily solved.

I'd like to conclude our discussion by turning to an underlying issue even more basic than poverty and more difficult to correct: greed.

Basic human greed lies behind many of our problems in health, making me realize that there is a spiritual dimension to the only ultimate solution. While I won't cease working and praying for that, there are some other steps we can take now. When I first entered medicine and for many years thereafter, I and most physicians did not expect to be paid for everything we did. Donating care to some people who couldn't afford it was something expected of the profession. All that vanished with the coming of entitlement programs like Medicare. We need to restore a sense of professionalism to medicine that includes the obligation, or really the opportunity, to provide donated care in appropriate situations. We also could be much more efficient in cracking down on fraud and abuse through stricter surveillance, tougher penalties, and legal protection for whistle-blowers. I'd rather see us ration greed than ration health care.

But greed is not limited to the purveyors of health care (physicians, pharmaceutical companies, hospitals, for example). Patients have also become too greedy—greedy for perfection, greedy for health, greedy even for life. Sometimes I think that Americans have forgotten that they must die of *something*.

I know, Tim, you often say that we put too much emphasis on curing, too little on *caring*. We need to do more about the times we cannot provide the cure but still can provide the care. Curing can cost billions; caring comes from the heart and soul.

Sincerely,
Chick

*

About the Authors

C. Everett Koop

Even as a young lad growing up in Brooklyn, C. Everett Koop wanted to become a physician. At age fourteen he sneaked into the operating theaters at the Columbia Presbyterian Medical Center to watch the surgeons. His first summer job, at age sixteen, was in the laboratory of another hospital, where he was soon performing urinalyses and blood counts and assisting the resident pathologist in performing autopsies.

It was at Dartmouth College that he acquired his nickname, Chick, and his medical degree. It was also where he met Betty, his wife of fifty-four years.

Because Dr. Koop achieved tremendous popularity as Surgeon General, it is easy to forget that prior to that appointment he had served for thirty-nine years as a pediatric surgeon. Trained in the 1940s under the watchful eyes of some of the medical profession's most prominent surgeons, Dr. Koop was one of the pioneers in the developing specialty of children's surgery. He was instrumental in developing procedures for neonatal surgery and undertook countless surgical cases that others had deemed hopeless.

One Sunday shortly after being appointed surgeon-in-chief at Children's Hospital of Philadelphia, Dr. Koop completed his rounds, walked a few blocks north of the hospital to Tenth Presbyterian Church, and slipped into the balcony. The preaching of the church's minister, Donald Grey Barnhouse, compelled Koop to return Sunday after Sunday until one day the message of the Gospel reached him in such a way that he became a believer.

Dr. Koop's tenure as Surgeon General included highly-publicized campaigns against smoking and pleas for honest information and education about AIDS. He has also been a vocal advocate of the sanctity of human life and a critic of any health-care system that does not provide basic services to rich and poor alike. Since leaving the office of Surgeon General, Dr. Koop has maintained a busy schedule that includes writing, speaking, and teaching. He is a Distinguished Scholar to the Carnegie Foundation, and at Dartmouth he is the McInerney Professor of Surgery and Senior Scholar at the C. Everett Koop Institute. He lives in Bethesda, Maryland.

Timothy Johnson

While growing up in Rockford, Illinois, Tim Johnson was active in communications activities as a member of the debate team and editor of his high school newspaper. At Augustana College in nearby Rock Island he majored in history with a minor in philosophy and took the bare minimum of science courses required for medical school.

After college, Dr. Johnson entered his denomination's seminary, North Park, in Chicago. During this period he met Nancy, his wife of twenty-nine years, who was then a student nurse. While in seminary his interest in medicine intensified, and two years after graduating he entered medical school in Albany, New York. After obtaining his medical degree he specialized in the then-new field of emergency medicine and became director of emergency medicine at a Boston area hospital. He also taught emergency medicine at Massachusetts General Hospital in Boston.

During that time in the early 1970s he became acquainted with the general director of Massachusetts General Hospital, Dr. John Knowles, who was also part owner of the ABC affiliate in Boston, WCVB. Dr. Knowles was instrumental in convincing Dr. Johnson to do some part-time television work for the station, which led to his association with "Good Morning America" in 1975.

During the next ten years Dr. Johnson made a gradual transition from full-time clinical practice to full-time television work when he became medical editor for ABC News in 1984. He also obtained a master's degree from Harvard School of Public Health and became the founding editor for the Harvard Medical School Health Letter.

Today, Dr. Johnson continues to reside in the Boston area and spends the majority of his time in his work for ABC. He also serves as a volunteer member of the pastoral staff of his church.